Published by
Lion Books
Part of the SPCK Group
SPCK, 36 Causton Street, London, SW1P 4ST
www.lionhudson.com

ISBN 978 0 74598 063 8
e-ISBN 978 0 74598 146 8

First edition 2021

Acknowledgments
Scripture quotations taken from The Holy Bible, New Revised Standard Version (Anglicized Edition), Oxford: Oxford University Press, 1995. All Bible quotes are from this version.

A catalogue record for this book is available from the British Library

Printed and bound in China, July 2021, LH25

THE STORY OF THE CROSS

A VISUAL HISTORY

MARTYN AND ESTHER WHITTOCK

DEDICATION

To my wonderful department and good friends Dee, Jon, Simon and Lewis. It is great to work with such dedicated people who have such a passion for delivering good quality Religious Studies teaching.

And to all my dear friends at Heart of England, especially: Liz, Richard, Craig, Linda, Jane, Kay, Rosie, Sarah, Swifty and Krystina. Thank you for the support, encouragement and laughter – particularly over the last (challenging) couple of years.

Esther Whittock

CONTENTS

ABOUT THE AUTHORS

Martyn Whittock graduated in Politics from Bristol University in 1980. He taught history for thirty-five years and latterly was curriculum leader for Spiritual, Moral, Social and Cultural Education at a Wiltshire secondary school. He is a Licensed Lay Minister in the Church of England. He has acted as a historical consultant to the National Trust and English Heritage. He retired from teaching in July 2016 to devote more time to writing.

He is the author or co-author of fifty-two books, including school history textbooks and adult history books. The latter include: *A Brief History of Life in the Middle Ages* (2009), *A Brief History of the Third Reich* (2011), *A Brief Guide to Celtic Myths and Legends* (2013), *The Viking Blitzkrieg AD 789–1098* (2013), *The Anglo-Saxon Avon Valley Frontier* (2014), *1016 and 1066: Why the Vikings Caused the Norman Conquest* (2016), *Norse Myths and Legends* (2017), *When God Was King* (2018), *The Vikings: From Odin to Christ* (2018), *Mayflower Lives* (2019), *Trump and the Puritans* (2020), *The Secret History of Soviet Russia's Police State* (2020). *When God was King* and *The Vikings* are published by Lion Hudson.

Also co-written with his youngest daughter, Esther, is *Christ: The First Two Thousand Years* (2016), *Daughters of Eve* (2021), and *Jesus the Unauthorized Biography* (2021). *The Story of the Cross* is their fourth collaborative venture. All these books are published by Lion Hudson.

Esther Whittock read Theology and Religious Studies at Jesus College, University of Cambridge, where she graduated with a First Class degree. She specialized in Christianity and biblical studies, focusing in her third year on Christology in the New Testament, the theology and composition of the Gospel of John, and the way that Christ and the Bible is understood in Indian and African cultures. Her work also included a study of the changes in the depiction of Christ's crucifixion over time. She also has an MA in Educational Leadership.

She is currently a secondary school teacher of Religious Studies at Heart of England School in the West Midlands; and previously she taught in an inner-city secondary school in Birmingham.

She is also the co-author of *Christ: The First Two Thousand Years* (2016), *Daughters of Eve* (2021), and *Jesus the Unauthorized Biography* (2021).

INTRODUCTION

The apostle Paul – writing to a group of early Christians living in the city of Corinth, in south-central Greece, in about AD 56 – sought to put into words something of the controversial nature of a core belief of the faith community they had joined. He wrote: "…we proclaim Christ crucified, a stumbling block to Jews and foolishness to Gentiles, but to those who are the called, both Jews and Greeks, Christ the power of God and the wisdom of God."[1]

He knew full well that to proclaim such a message to his contemporary society was to risk provoking both shock and ridicule in equal measure. Yet it was on this position that he took his stand and encouraged the Corinthians to do likewise.

In the twenty-first century it can be difficult to comprehend just how raw and radical (in the first century AD) was the Christian adherence to the idea that the looked-for messiah – whom Christians proclaim is the Son of God and one with the divinity of God – had been nailed to a cross. Some 2,000 years of artistic representation may have rather sanitized crucifixion at times. A moment's reflection is enough to realize its pain and horror; but this realization can still be rather crowded by images of empty crosses worked from gold and silver, by pictures of Jesus serenely gazing down from the cross, and by stained-glass portrayals that are certainly not stained by blood and sweat.

The cross, to many, was certainly both a stumbling-block and sheer foolishness. This was not how divinity behaved. This was not how divinity lived. This was certainly not how divinity died.

But the Corinthians had no such comforting assistance to reconcile them to the idea of crucifixion. They knew it all too well as the appallingly painful and humiliating form of execution that was favoured by the Roman state for those who incurred its condemnation and contempt. Some Corinthians had probably witnessed the crucifixion and death of criminals. Well-educated ones would have been aware of the fact that when the Greek-born Spartacus had led a slave revolt in Italy just over a century before, the revolt had ended with 6,000 captured slaves being crucified along the Appian Way leading from Rome to Capua. The cross was a criminal's death; a death befitting a rebel slave. It was designed to humiliate; it was designed to extend the process of execution; it was designed to deter. Looking now at a 4.5 inch (11 cm) Roman hand-forged nail we are reminded of the terrible mechanics of this form of dispatching the enemies of the state.

As if Christianity's claims regarding Christ being the Son of God were not shocking enough, the idea that such a focus of worship and devotion had died on a gibbet reserved for the lowest of the low only added to the incomprehension of many contemporaries, whether they were members of the Jewish community or Greeks. The cross, to many, was certainly both a stumbling-block and sheer foolishness. This was not how divinity behaved. This was not how divinity lived. This was certainly not how divinity died.

And yet the story of Christianity is very much the story of the cross over two millennia. It is that story that we will be exploring in this book; a story envisaged through the visual representations of the cross. In that story we will first see how contemporary culture responded to this shocking symbol. We will then explore how its presentation changed when the Roman Empire became Christian. We will meet trouser-wearing Viking representations of Christ, bound (rather than nailed) by plant tendrils. We will see the cross as a crusader symbol. We will explore the way in which the pain and agony was reinterpreted so as to show Christ reigning from his cross, only for this pain to be rediscovered in the later Middle Ages. We will see Christ on the cross as represented across varied times, cultures and ethnicities. In this process the cross became so engrained in concepts of sacrifice that it has dominated military awards for courage.

However, we will also see it as envisaged in high-end jewellery and in controversial performance art. We will see it manipulated and abused by violent nationalists seeking to impose their racial vision and prejudices on others. We will see it presented as a self-defining statement by some of the poorest and most downtrodden communities, who have recognized their humiliation – and also their hope – reflected in Christ who died like a marginalized criminal. Whether pondered by those of Christian faith, other faiths or no religious faith, the cross continues to provoke questions, while also now being engrained in worldwide culture as exhibited in national flags and military awards. It is immediately recognizable as a defining symbol in religious terms, but is also embraced by secular society as an appealing shape and form.

Despite this, the cross – when associated with Christ's death – has not ceased to shock and challenge. It is still a symbol that both unites and divides people. Despite all the superb art and exquisite jewellery it has inspired, the cross of Christ remains a symbol of execution. It is more than a logo; more than an internationally recognized brand. It is a defining statement of belief which is, at times, as bitterly opposed in the twenty-first century as it was in the first centuries of Christianity. When twenty-one Egyptian Coptic Christians were martyred by members of ISIS on a Libyan beach in February 2015, the video released by their killers described those beheaded as "people of the cross". Indeed they were. But *why* they were is the subject of this book.

Chapter 1

THE CROSS OF SHAME

The cross – whether carrying the body of Christ as a crucifix or as a simple empty shape – is the globally recognized symbol of Christianity. It appears in churches and in pop art. It is worn by millions as a fashion accessory. It appears on flags as varied as the Union Flag of the United Kingdom and the Royal Standard of Tonga; and every single Scandinavian flag carries it. It has morphed into secular forms such as the Victoria Cross, the *Croix de Guerre* and the Iron Cross, or the badge of the International Red Cross. The last named, though, has its Christian origins (via a reversal of the colours of the Swiss flag) recognized in that its Islamic equivalent is the Red Crescent.

Since it was the day of Preparation, the Jews did not want the bodies left on the cross during the sabbath, especially because that sabbath was a day of great solemnity. So they asked Pilate to have the legs of the crucified men broken and the bodies removed. Then the soldiers came and broke the legs of the first and of the other who had been crucified with him.

John 19:31-32

All of this means that it can be easy to lose sight of the fact that the cross started as a form of execution devised for its infliction of drawn-out pain and humiliation. It is hard to imagine mass-produced jewellery or high art based on an electric chair, a lethal-injection syringe or a noose. This makes the cross a particularly intriguing image to trace across history. As a religious, cultural and fashion item it has few parallels in its curious blend of atrocity, simplicity and global brand. It is a story that is 2,000 years old and, in that time, there have been dramatic changes, developments, twists and turns in how people have understood it, represented it, responded to it and used it. This book is an overview of that "story", and the course of it is signposted by a number of striking images that testify to the twists and turns of that journey through time. They are chosen from across continents and cultures, as well as across centuries. Each one has been selected to reflect a stage in the development of the story. That is why this exploration is called *The Story of the Cross*.

A humiliating and brutal form of execution

The 2,000-year-old story of the cross as a Christian symbol begins in the Roman province of Judea under Roman occupation in the first half of the first century AD. But that cross had a backstory. Darius I of Persia used crucifixion as a punishment for political opponents in the sixth century BC, according to the later Greek historian Herodotus. Alexander the Great and the Carthaginians of North Africa employed it too. From these uses it was adopted under the Roman Republic and later Empire as a suitable punishment for slaves, non-citizens or citizens found guilty of treason. When the slave revolt of Spartacus was defeated in 71 BC the Roman general, Crassus, crucified 6,000 prisoners from the army of ex-slaves. The avenue of the dead and dying lined the Appian Way from Rome to Capua.

Contrary to popular belief, the Old Testament judgment that "anyone hung on a tree is under God's curse" (Deuteronomy 21:23) does not refer to crucifixion, since the reference probably implies that the criminal was already dead; and "hung on a tree" suggests the display of a dead body, not the nailing of a body to wood. Nevertheless, it is easy to see that when Greek and Roman rulers introduced crucifixion to the Jewish communities, its shame and humiliation resonated with an existing mindset. Crucifixion was as shameful as it was agonizing.

Picture 1.1
The crucified ankle bone of "Yehohanan, son of Hagakol" or "Yehohanan, son of the Crucified One", first century AD (pre-AD 70). The Israel Museum, Jerusalem.

We know that the Roman occupying power used crucifixion as a punishment in the province of Judea through a shocking archaeological find. In 1968, the Israeli Department of Antiquities excavated a series of tombs at Giv'at ha-Mivtar, north of the walled city of Jerusalem. There they discovered the first (and so far only) archaeological evidence of the use of crucifixion. They found a stone box containing human bones: an ossuary. Scratched into the side of the box were the words: "Yehohanan, son of Hagakol". Inside the box the archaeologists found a heel bone with an iron nail driven through it *(Picture1.1)*. The ossuary also contained the bones of a child, aged three or four years of age. Some experts believe that "Hagakol" was not a personal name, but instead was a term meaning "crucified". In which case, the inscription should be read as: "Yehohanan, son of the Crucified One". If so, Yehohanan was the child's name.[1] The matter remains open to debate.

The manner of death in crucifixion was terrible. Unless the body was supported in some way, the full weight of the victim hung from the arms (whether bound or nailed), and death from muscular spasms and asphyxia would occur within two or three hours. As the victim grew weaker it would prove harder for them to pull themselves up on their arms in order to breathe. To prolong the agony, the Romans sometimes added a small seat (pointed to add additional pain) to give the body some support; at other times a foot support was added. In these cases, it could take as long as three days for the victim to die.

In the case of the victim in the Jerusalem ossuary, it seems that the nail bent as it hit a knot in the wood (a piece of olive wood was found on the tip of the nail). The bent nail was hard to remove after death, so the entire foot was hacked off but kept with the body. A small plaque of wood (either acacia or pistacia wood) survived between the head of the nail and the bone – probably there to prevent the foot from tearing free of the nail. Initial study of the bones suggested that the actual position on the cross was formed by twisting both legs to one side (with the knees bent) and putting a single large nail through both heel bones to fix them to the front of the cross. This would have formed a semi-sitting position with the man's body twisted to one side. There must have been some support under the victim in order to prevent the collapse of the body and to prolong the agony. A scratch on one bone of the right forearm seemed to indicate that his arms were nailed to the horizontal bar and that the nail was driven in just above the wrist. It seemed that the man's legs were finally brutally broken, in order to accelerate death.[2] This is what the Gospel of John describes as happening to the two criminals crucified with Jesus (John 19:31–32).

Some of these conclusions have been challenged, with some experts later arguing that the heels were actually nailed separately to either side of the upright post and questioning whether the arms were nailed and the legs

Picture 1.2

"Alexamenos worships [his] God", c. 200. Palatine Hill Museum, Rome.

broken.[3] The arms may have been tied – instead of nailed – to the cross-beam and Roman writings refer to both practices. One piece of graffito from Pompeii, Italy, reads: "May you be *nailed* to the cross!", while another says: "Get *hung*!"[4] Other references refer to nails and/or ropes being variously used. There clearly was variety and we should not expect uniformity in an execution method carried out across a wide period of time and in many different situations. Whatever the exact method of fixing and the position of the body, the death was agonizing. It was not nailing but asphyxiation that killed a crucifixion victim.

The account of Jesus' death in John's Gospel says that his "hands" were nailed as well as his feet. However, it should be remembered that the Greek word used in the New Testament could describe the wrists as well as the hands, and Jesus' arms may have been both tied to give support to the body and nailed (through either wrists or hands).[5] The same word translated as "hands" in John is translated as "wrists" when later describing where chains were fixed on the apostle Peter.[6] This, along with the fact that the New Testament never describes the cross in detail, or exactly how Jesus was placed on it, means that over 2,000 years it has been artistically represented in a number of ways.

Under the Roman Empire, at the time of Jesus, huge numbers of people suffered this form of execution. In AD 7 a rebellion occurred in Judea following the death of King Herod. After its suppression, the Roman legate of Syria, Quintilius Varus, crucified 2,000 Jews in Jerusalem. In AD 70 the Roman general, Titus, crucified somewhere in the region of 500 Jews a day over several months during the siege of Jerusalem, following a widespread revolt against Roman rule.

"Alexamenos worships [his] God"

It is clear from this that non-Christians of the first and second centuries AD – Jews, Greeks, Romans and others – would have been very puzzled indeed by the idea of crucifixion as an honourable religious symbol or as the defining feature of a deity. We can see this in the earliest surviving picture of the crucifixion *(Picture 1.2)*. It dates from about the year 200 and was found on the Palatine Hill, in Rome. It was not made by Christians and it was not created to adorn a church or be worn as an item of devotion. It was an example of graffiti designed to offend. A human figure raises a hand in worship to a figure naked on a cross; the crucified figure is depicted with the head of a donkey. Below the crude sketch these words are scratched in Greek: "*Alexamenos sebete theon*",[7] which, despite some complications in the hastily written Greek, is most convincingly translated as "Alexamenos worships [his] God".[8]

We do not know who scratched it into the wall and, similarly, we do not know who Alexamenos was. What is clear is that the person who produced this graffito was mocking Alexamenos and his Christian beliefs. It is a reminder of how shameful a death crucifixion was in the Roman Empire and the controversial nature of a religion that declared its God had been nailed to a cross. Clearly, whoever carved this graffito thought the whole thing contemptible. Hence the donkey head placed on the crucified figure.

It is thought that the wall bearing this scratched portrayal was part of the Paedagogium, a school to train servants in the imperial household of the Roman emperor. The Palatine Hill in Rome was where a number of Roman emperors built residences; indeed the name gave us the modern word "palace". At that point in time the imperial household and the official religion of the empire was polytheistic (worshipping many gods/goddesses). One can only assume that Alexamenos was one of the growing minority of Christians and, probably, was one of the imperial servants.

Whatever the exact method of fixing and the position of the body, the death was agonizing. It was not nailing but asphyxiation that killed a crucifixion victim.

Intriguingly, in the next-door building, another piece of graffito was found, but written by a different hand. Scratched on the wall plaster, in Latin this time, are the words "*Alexamenos fidelis*" ("Alexamenos the faithful").[9] It looks as though either Alexamenos or an ally did not take the insult scratched on the wall in the other room lying down. Or it might have been yet another attempt to identify and therefore denounce Alexamenos as a Christian.

The shape of the cross is interesting. It is in the shape of a "T" (sometimes referred to as a Tau Cross, after the nineteenth letter of the Greek alphabet that it resembles) and it has not yet developed into the more familiar Latin Cross (a cross where the upright arm extends above the crossbar). It is possible that the Tau Cross was the shape more usually employed in executions across the empire, or it may simply have been the type of gibbet with which the graffiti artist was more familiar in Rome. He clearly had seen such executions, since the platform on which the feet rest and the ropes used to bind the victim to the cross-beam are likely to have been used in real executions, as we have already seen, in order to prolong the agony of the person crucified.

Looking closely at the graffito it seems as if the scene is being portrayed from behind, since the T-shaped cross can be seen superimposed on the body. However, there is a break in the upright at the lower back. This may have been an error in a swiftly scratched insult, or it could imply impaling, which was occasionally also done in this form of execution. If the latter, there is not the slightest hint of this in the gospel accounts and it may simply have been a variant of this method of execution that had been witnessed by the anonymous artist.

This is the beginning of the story of portraying the cross – a beginning that is both shocking and controversial. To many people living in the first and second centuries AD the cross was a shameful image.

Picture 1.3

Crucifixion scene, from the TV mini series *Jesus of Nazareth*, released in 1977. In modern films the brutal reality of crucifixion is clearly portrayed.

Chapter 2

PEOPLE OF THE CROSS

The fact that Jesus died on a cross left early Christians with a challenge. How were they to understand these events? And, given the extremely negative view of crucifixion in the Roman Empire, how were they to explain this to others? It would have been challenge enough if Jesus had died in a manner considered noble and honourable to explain why the messiah (in Greek: Christ) had been rejected by the leaders of his own people and executed by an alien power. But on a cross? Of all forms of execution it was the one most associated with contempt and humiliation in their contemporary society. This was indeed a challenge. But it was one that early Christians embraced to such a degree that it rapidly became the centrepiece of their explanation of the love of God and the mission of Jesus; and later it would become one of the defining symbols by which they would be identified. From the earliest times this group of people would be "people of the cross", but it took a while for the symbol itself to be deployed as a defining emblem. The first ideas about the cross appear in the New Testament and these ideas then informed later representations.

The cross in the writings of Paul

Paul (originally named Saul) was a well-educated and well-connected Jewish intellectual who was a persecutor of early Christians. He was transformed into an enthusiastic exponent of the new faith by a conversion experience while going to organize further repression in Damascus. It was Paul who expressed many of the early faith statements of Christian thought as he wrote letters to early Christian communities in what is now Turkey and Greece. He wrote these before the first gospels were written. Consequently, it is in Paul's letters that we first get an idea of how early Christians understood the cross.

In essence, Paul wrote that the cross overturns human standards and expectations. This would certainly have rung true in the first-century

Roman Empire. Its "power" seemed "weakness" to people, but that, according to Paul, was how God revealed himself and set out a new kind of wisdom and way of reconciling people to himself. Paul wrote: "Christ crucified, a stumbling block to Jews and foolishness to Gentiles, but to those who are the called, both Jews and Greeks, Christ the power of God and the wisdom of God."[1] According to Paul, God deliberately chose a way of death that was socially unacceptable in order to show the futility of what the world thinks is wise and strong. And in choosing such a despised way of dying, God reached out to the despised and rejected.[2] At the cross Jews and Gentiles were reconciled.[3] For Paul, it was on the cross that Jesus took on himself the punishment that humans deserve for their wrongdoing, and therefore made it possible to be reconciled to God. In this way the cross became a powerful symbol of reconciliation and hope. It was also a powerful symbol of how Jesus' followers should be humble and ready to suffer for their faith too.

Early Christians, who were still sensitive to the stigma attached to the cross itself, could therefore focus on it without embarrassment. Despite this, it was still some time (perhaps two centuries) before such a symbol would be openly displayed as a defining "badge". An early example of this can be seen in the depiction of a cross-anchor and fish on a third-century tombstone from the Catacombs of Priscilla, in Rome *(Picture 2.1)*. Here the cross has become an anchor (symbolizing hope) and, alongside the

Picture 2.1
Cross-anchor and fishes on a tombstone from the Catacombs of Priscilla, Rome, third century.

Christian symbol of the fish, was adapted as an acceptable statement of Christian faith. But it took a long time to reach even that carefully adapted emblem.

The cross in the preaching of Peter in the book of Acts

Paul was not the only person articulating Christian ideas about the cross. The book of Acts contains speeches reflecting faith statements of the earliest Christians. It may have been written around the year 70, at about the same time as the gospels, and the evidence suggests that its writer was the same man who wrote the Gospel of Luke.

The earliest example of Christian preaching in Acts is that of Peter, preaching to the crowds on the Day of Pentecost. Peter would have been well aware of how his listeners regarded crucifixion, but he used it as a way of making two dramatic points: first, he said that those listening were guilty of rejecting God's messiah because "you crucified and killed [Jesus] by the hands of those outside the law [the Romans]" but, secondly, even such a terrible death had been used by God, since "God raised him up, having freed him from death, because it was impossible for him to be held in its power".[4] In this way the cross revealed the cost of salvation and the eventual vindication of Jesus by God. The minimalist way Peter did this suggests there was still a rawness over such a death, but reveals that (as with Paul's letters) *this* cross was a revolutionary new beginning.

The cross in the gospels

Many modern experts believe that the Gospel of Mark was the first gospel to be written, around the year 70, with the Gospel of Matthew and the Gospel of Luke being composed sometime in the 80s. The Gospel of John is very different from the other three. This gospel focuses on a narrower set of events and themes than the other gospels, and most of it recounts the events leading to the death of Jesus. This gospel could have been compiled any time between about 70 and 100.

Looking back on the events at the end of Jesus' life, the gospel writers saw in the cross the dramatic reason for that life. So Matthew, Mark and Luke record Jesus saying that "whoever does not take up the cross and follow me is not worthy of me".[5] In John's Gospel a new understanding of the messiah-king is apparent when "Pilate also had an inscription written and put on the cross. It read, 'Jesus of Nazareth, the King of the Jews'".[6] For the gospel writers the cross was the culmination of Jesus' life and not an unforeseen disaster; and his death on it was vindicated by his resurrection three days later.

The cross in the early church community

For 300 years after the death of Jesus, Christians preached about his death but were clearly reluctant to depict it in art. At a time when people were still being crucified (it continued to be used for executions until the time of the first Christian emperor, Constantine I, in the fourth century) the image was probably too controversial. The lack of evidence for early Christian depictions of the cross clearly later frustrated somebody enough to forge one. The *Orpheos Bakkikos* was purchased in Italy, studied in 1922 and housed at the Kaiser Friedrich Museum in Berlin, until being lost during the Second World War *(Picture 2.2)*. It purports to be a Roman magical talisman in which the maker sought to harness the cross (so central to Christian beliefs) by linking it to the pagan belief in Orpheus and Bacchus, to produce an item probably thought to have magic powers. The amulet was denounced as a fake in 1926, but continues to appear in some studies of Roman art.[7] That such magical talismans depicting the cross existed is beyond dispute though. A genuine one, carved in jasper, dates from perhaps as early as the second century and shows a naked, long-haired, bearded man tied to a tall cross and surrounded by Greek letters that read: "Son", "Father", "Jesus Christ" and variations on "Jesus" and "Emmanuel" *(Picture 2.3)*. The repetition of the words suggests that they were thought to have magical significance, and in the British Museum it is classified as a "magical gem".[8] Clearly, mainstream

Picture 2.2

Orpheos Bakkikos talisman. Kaiser Friedrich Museum in Berlin, but lost in the Second World War.

Picture 2.3
"Magical gem", second to third century. British Museum, London.

Christians did not yet feel comfortable about depicting the cross, and such depictions were the preserve of fringe activities.

However, in time, as crucifixion ceased to be a common form of execution, the cross started to be displayed visually in Christian art. One of the earliest examples may date from as early as the third century: the *Constanţa Intaglio*, made from a gemstone called carnelian *(Picture 2.4)*. Found in Romania, it shows a naked figure of Jesus on a T-cross with the twelve apostles (six either side). As is usual in these early depictions he stands with legs straight down, not flexed as in later depictions; and, also found on other early crosses, his arms appear bound to the cross, not nailed. In Greek letters around the top is the abbreviated form of: "Jesus Christ Son of God Saviour".

From this period onwards depictions of the cross became part of the mainstream, with the earliest manuscript picture appearing in the Syriac *Rabbula Gospels*, in about 586 *(Picture 2.5)*. In this depiction a clothed and straight-legged Jesus is clearly nailed to the cross. Jesus gazes down to the haloed figure of his mother, Mary. A pattern of presenting the cross that would be common for over half a millennium was finally in place.

Picture 2.4
Constanța Intaglio, third to fourth century. The British Museum, London.

Picture 2.5

Earliest known illuminated manuscript depiction of the crucifixion, from the Syriac *Rabbula Gospels*, sixth century. Biblioteca Mediceo Laurenziana, Florence.

Chapter 3

"BY THIS CONQUER!"

According to one tradition, which was recorded by the Christian historian Eusebius of Caesarea twenty-five years after the event,[1] in the year 312, during a civil war over control of the Roman Empire, one of the central contenders – Constantine – saw a noontime vision. In it he witnessed a cross placed over the sun and saw the words "By this conquer!" Christ then appeared to him that night in a dream, along with the same sign of the cross.

The cross was, as we have seen, the dramatic and also very controversial symbol of Christ's crucifixion. By the early fourth century it was well known as a symbol of the Christian faith, but one whose explicit visual portrayal was still not widespread and a little hesitant in an empire where Christians still faced periodic persecution at the hands of the Roman state. Indeed, this had occurred only as recently as the 250s, in the reigns of Decius and Valerian; and then most violently during the reign of the emperor Diocletian and his successors, starting in 303 and lasting until 313 (the Edict of Milan). It was, therefore, very recently that Christians had been martyred at the hands of the Roman state (at least in its eastern half). Outside the Roman Empire, large numbers of Christians were to die for the faith in the Persian Sassanid Empire in the 340s. Consequently, martyrdom was a contemporary experience, so the cross as a form of Roman-sponsored execution would have remained a very controversial symbol.

Considering this, its role within the career of the man who would become the first Christian emperor was remarkable. An earlier tradition than the one recorded by Eusebius described how, in a dream, Constantine was commanded to use a different sign in battle to ensure victory. This account was written by the Roman historian Lactantius,[2] and his description suggests that the sign was related to the "*Chi-Rho*" symbol (the combined first two letters of "Christ" in Greek:[3] *XP*) that was painted on the shields of Constantine's soldiers. That this involved the Greek letter *chi* (*X*) would have also brought to mind the symbol of the cross. Alternatively, it may have been the so-called *Staurogram* or *Tau-Rho* (formed from the Greek letters *T* and *P*),[4] which was used to abbreviate the

Greek word *stauros* (a word for cross) and may actually have been taken as a visual representation of Christ on the cross. The similarity between the Greek letter T and some early representations of the cross is striking.[5]

Constantine defeated his enemy Maxentius at the battle of the Milvian Bridge, and became emperor. Whatever the truth of these visionary traditions, the cross of Christ and the title of Christ had been dramatically imposed on the politics and state of the Roman Empire.[6]

Victorious in this battle, Constantine went on to become the first Christian emperor of the Roman Empire. By 324 Constantine was sole ruler of that empire, Christianity was his favoured religion and his commitment to the faith was clear. His reign ushered in a new era in the history of Christianity and a new chapter of the story of the cross. Having started as a symbol of humiliation and shame, the cross was soon to become the symbol of a Christian empire that had originally crucified Christ. It was a dramatic development and one that was soon reflected in the way the cross was depicted and presented.

The "True Cross" was even (allegedly) found by Constantine's mother, Helena, in a fourth-century archaeological dig. It was during the reign of Constantine that the "Holy Sepulchre" (the place of Christ's burial and resurrection) was apparently found in Jerusalem in 325, after pagan temples there were demolished. In 335 the newly constructed Church of the Holy Sepulchre was inaugurated. The "True Cross", on which Christ died, was allegedly discovered at the same time as this building work occurred. This is highly unlikely, given that the original object was the property of the pagan Roman state, and the early church was a politically powerless minority. How such a group could have gained possession of the means of execution of Christ is difficult to imagine and says more about a later cult of relics than it does about first-century realities. But this object became a source of treasured wooden relics. Within Rome, for example, Constantine preserved a piece within a jewelled reliquary in a specially built church, and Pope Hilarus (461–68) had the oratory of the Holy Cross built to preserve another fragment. Pieces of the "True Cross" would be venerated across western Europe for the next millennium.[7]

It should be noted that Jerusalem had ceased to be a Jewish city after the crushing of the Bar Kokhba revolt against Roman rule in 135. In 335 it became, in effect, a Christian city. The "discovery" of the cross of Christ by Helena played a central part in this reinvention of Jerusalem.

The cross in a newly Christian Roman Empire – and beyond

The traditions associated with the victory of Constantine clearly caught people's imagination. On the so-called Passion Sarcophagus – probably from the Catacomb of Domitilla, Rome, and dating from c. 350 – the central

carving of Christ's cross merges into Constantine's *Chi-Rho* standard *(Picture 3.1)*. On either side of this powerful symbolism we see, from left to right, the biblical scenes of Simon of Cyrene carrying the cross; Christ crowned with thorns; then the cross and the *Chi-Rho* within a wreath of victory; and, finally, Christ before Pontius Pilate. While this shows nothing of the violence and humiliation of the act of crucifixion, the symbol itself is centre-stage and the events leading up to it are clearly identified. However, we might conclude that it is the very absence of the realities of crucifixion that has made this display acceptable. An empty cross was easier to depict than a person fixed to it. It would take some time for that to be acceptable. And in the meantime the empty cross was a perfectly valid symbol, since its emptiness reminded viewers of the resurrection victory that came later, by which time the cross itself was, of course, empty. This is the case in this example, since the resting soldier and the sleeping soldier at the foot of the cross clearly recall the guards from the gospel accounts of Easter morning.

Picture 3.1
Chi-Rho symbol and cross, and scenes from the Passion of Christ, on the Passion Sarcophagus c. 350. Museo Pio Christiano, Vatican Museums, Rome.

The association of the cross with imperial rule appealed to the so-called barbarians who lived beyond the borders of the empire and later invaded. It was both a political and a religious symbol associated with Rome. In fact the

Picture 3.2

The first use of a Christian cross on a coin. From the Aksumite kingdom of Ethiopia, during the reign of King Ezana II (320s–c. 360).

first appearance of the cross on a coin comes from the Aksumite kingdom of Ethiopia in present-day Ethiopia and Eritrea, in the reign of King Ezana II (320s–c. 360), who began to feature the cross on his coins. It was the first time that the Christian cross had ever featured on coinage *(Picture 3.2)*. King Ezana II was converted to Christianity in 324, through his Greek slave-teacher Frumentius. Alongside Constantine the Great of Rome and Tiridates of Armenia, King Ezana was one of the first rulers to convert to Christianity and he made this clear on his coinage.

This African ruler was a trailblazer of a trend that would soon also be seen in the successor states of western Europe, where other kings, such as those in Anglo-Saxon England, would also place crosses on their coinage. But this iconographic trend had first occurred in Africa. We will explore more of this in Chapter 5.

The symbol of the empty cross became prominent from the mid-fourth century onwards. And it was increasingly associated with imperial and kingly power as both a way of communicating the Christian allegiance of the (now Christian) empire and successor states, and in claiming Christ's power, authority and legitimacy for the ruler. This became particularly the case in the eastern (Byzantine) empire that survived the fall of Rome to the barbarians and which continued in existence until the Islamic conquest of Constantinople in 1453. Here the emperor came to represent an intense

Picture 3.3

Christ and crosses on gold Byzantine coin (*solidus*) of the emperor Basil I. Minted in Constantinople, c. 868–70.

Picture 3.4

Georgian Eastern Orthodox pectoral cross from Martvili (eighth to ninth century). Figures of Christ and the Virgin Mary in gold repoussé, with enamel, pearls and precious stones. Tbilisi National Museum of Art and History, Tbilisi.

sacred authority whose prestige and mystique was enhanced by his role of representing Christ's authority on earth. In this context, images of the cross became closely entwined with imperial power. This was readily communicated across the eastern empire on, for example, its coins *(Picture 3.3)*. On this gold *solidus* of the emperor Basil I (dating from c. 868–70) we see on the obverse Christ seated facing us on his throne. His halo is characteristically marked by a cross. On the reverse stands Emperor Basil I and his son Constantine, with a patriarchal cross between them. In addition, each wears a crown surmounted by a cross. Four crosses on one coin. Clearly the cross was intimately linked to their imperial rule. It was *the* badge and symbol that represented their source of authority (the patriarchal cross of the church) and their right to exercise rule on behalf of God (the cross-surmounted crown). Other rulers came to imitate such regal uses of the cross.

Within the Eastern Orthodox Church, the splendid grandeur of this imperial understanding can be seen on the eighth- to ninth-century pectoral cross from Martvili in Georgia, which removed all violence from the representation *(Picture 3.4)*. Instead, we see Christ and the Virgin Mary serenely superimposed on a gold cross and surrounded by pearls and precious stones. It is comparable with the best products of Byzantine imperial workmanship. In such a presentation Christ was not represented as suffering on the cross but rather as reigning from it in the company of the Virgin. And it is to this striking theme of reigning from the cross – even when depicting actual crucifixion – that we now turn.

Chapter 4

REIGNING FROM THE CROSS

We have seen how the first recorded depiction of the crucifixion was a mockery of it. Yet this symbol of degradation and scandal became a symbol of Christianity. In this process the cross and the crucifix lost their shameful connotations and proclaimed a message of redemption. As we have seen, it was not until after the reign of Constantine the Great that crucifixion images appeared; before then it was simply the cross, rather than Jesus dying on the cross, that was displayed (and even this depiction was tentative at first). Then, from the fifth century onwards, the focus shifted from the instrument of death to both the instrument and the dying person. The crucifix image appeared. But as it did so it became clear that the early crucifix was a symbol of

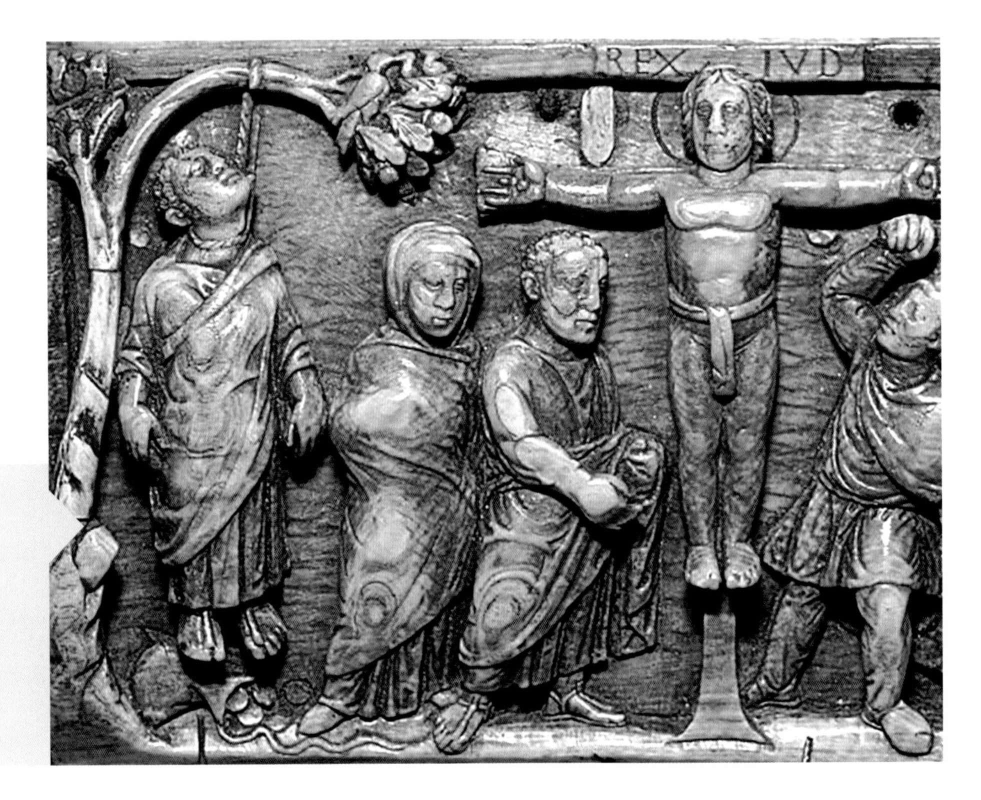

Picture 4.1
Panel from an *Ivory Casket: The Crucifixion of Christ.* Probably made in Rome, c. 420–30. British Museum, London.

victory rather than of suffering. Christ was *reigning* from the cross rather than *suffering* on the cross.

Christus triumphans

One of the earliest surviving Christian crucifix images is an ivory relief dating from c. 420 *(Picture 4.1)*. On it Jesus is calm and alive – illustrated by his open eyes – and reigning from the cross. The divinity of Christ is expressed through physical strength and determination to endure such pain. Here Jesus is seen not as passive in his death but instead he chooses to die; he has power and is in control. This view of Christ echoes verses found in the Gospel of John: "I am the good shepherd… And I lay down my life for the sheep… I lay it down of my own accord" (John 10:14–18). The ivory relief communicates the idea that this was not a moment of human weakness but of divine victory for Christ. Such depictions reveal a confident faith in Christ's godly nature, his mission of redemption and his completion of God's divine plan. Such a depiction of Christ may also have been a reaction to opposition from both pagans and Jews who contested the belief that Christ was divine and all-powerful.

By the early medieval period, hymns too demonstrated this triumphant Christ. The hymn *Vexilla Regis* (*The Banners of the King*), attributed to Venantius Fortunatus, bishop of Poitiers, in the sixth century, and written for a relic of the "True Cross", likewise celebrates the crucified Christ as a successful king hailing him as, "God ruling the nations from a tree".[1]

In this period, the cross appears to equip Christ for battle – the battle against the power of death. We will shortly see echoes of this in the Anglo-Saxon poem *The Dream of the Rood* (Chapter 5). This cross brings life and this is more apparent than death in these depictions. Overall, it is not the method of death but rather the event of the death (and its outcome) that is important in these depictions. In these images of what became known as *Christus triumphans* (triumphant Christ), the focus was not on showing historical realism but on demonstrating the divinity of Christ and stating that his victorious death leads to the salvation of humanity.[2]

Picture 4.2

Cross of Otto and Mathilde, late tenth century. Essen Cathedral Treasury.

Picture 4.3
Gero Cross, late tenth century. Cologne Cathedral.

The crux gemmata

Consistent with this emphasis in the early medieval period, the crucifix was often transformed into the *crux gemmata* (jewelled cross), encrusted with jewels and precious metals, which demonstrated Christ's regal nature.[3] There was a strong relationship between this and the Imperial Christ depicted in Byzantine imagery and icons (see Chapter 3). The *Cross of Otto and Mathilde*, from the late tenth century (made sometime between 973 and 982, and now kept in the Essen Cathedral Treasury), is a good example of this, with its depiction of the crucified Christ on a golden cross, surrounded by richly coloured gems *(Picture 4.2)*.[4] The development of the *crux gemmata* reflected the continued understanding of the cross as a symbol of honour, while also presenting Christ's death as an idealized event that promised future glory for all believers. The figure of Christ, glorious in his death, had now become the dogmatic focal point and this came to dominate most early medieval depictions. Similarly, contemporary Christian icons of Christ and the Virgin Mary also displayed their majesty.

The cross of death and beauty

These crucifixes encouraged the viewer to find majestic beauty and celebration in the death of Jesus. St Augustine had early stated that Christ was "beautiful in his flagellation, beautiful giving up his Spirit… beautiful on the cross".[5] While the act of crucifixion in and of itself was undeniably ugly and offensive, this understanding presented the death of Jesus as glorious and good, and as the means of delivering humanity from their sins. It was this that was taken on board by the writer of *Vexilla Regis* and by the craftspeople who constructed a *crux gemmata*. And this was a royal triumph that could become the possession of believers as they identified with both the royal cross and the resurrection that followed. In short, it emphasized the belief that the story did not end at Christ's death, but his death was a route to resurrection victory. In this sense the cross became a thing of beauty, as the gold and jewels of the *crux gemmata* proclaimed.

This juxtaposition of death and beauty is demonstrated by the *Gero Cross* in Cologne Cathedral, which was made c. 965–70 *(Picture 4.3)*. It is a striking depiction of Christ, and probably the oldest Western depiction of a dead Christ on the cross; most previous depictions show the crucified Christ with his head up and looking straight ahead. In contrast, this piece emphasizes the sacrificial death of Christ, since it shows his hanging head with eyes closed, and a lifeless body.[6] Yet while the figure is mortal and vulnerable, the golden halo, the gilding and absence of damage to the body give serenity even to the depiction of death itself. It mixes both humanity and divinity, proclaiming belief in the Son of God who victoriously overcame death for the redemption of human beings. In this way the sculptor "fittingly contrives to suggest the noble and dignified God-man whose humility in subjecting himself to this ordeal paradoxically underlined his divinity".[7] So, on the *Gero Cross*, even in death Christ reigns from the cross.

"The Smiling Christ" on the cross

So far, it is Christ in his royal majesty and in his victorious death that has characterized these images of reigning from the cross. The thirteenth-century depiction of Christ from the chapel in the Castle of St Francis Xavier in Spain takes this further in a depiction that has been termed "The Smiling Christ" *(Picture 4.4)*. It shows Christ looking serene and peaceful on the cross.[8] Even though he is clearly nailed to the cross, stripped, and wearing a crown of thorns, it is the control of Christ over the situation (even of death itself) that is emphasized. This again is reflective of the account of Jesus' death found in John's Gospel, which states that "he [Jesus] said, 'It is finished.' Then he bowed his head and gave up his spirit" (John 19:30). The "Smiling Christ" who is depicted as smiling, even at the point of death, communicates a belief in one who does not fear death.[9] It is possible to surmise that in such a depiction Christ was envisaged as anticipating his resurrection. A similar calm approach to their own death was therefore encouraged among those who viewed such an image.

Calm regality was the characteristic feature of this representation in its different forms. In the earliest depictions (such as in the jewelled crosses) this accompanied an emphasis on the conjoined divinity and humanity of Christ. In the later depictions (such as in the *Gero Cross* and "The Smiling Christ") the emphasis is more on serenity in the face of death, and the confidence this could evoke in the believer. Both, though, stressed Christ's death as victorious and the cross as a symbol of victory and life. Whether alive or dead, such a Christ was *Christus triumphans* and reigning from his cross.

Picture 4.4

"The Smiling Christ", thirteenth century. Chapel of the Castle of St Francis Xavier, Navarra.

Chapter 5

THE CROSS AND THE INHERITORS OF ROME

The Roman Empire collapsed in western Europe in the fifth century AD. In 410 Rome was sacked by invading barbarians and in 476 the last western emperor – Romulus Augustulus – was deposed by the commander of his own Germanic mercenary troops. In the east the Byzantine Empire, based on Constantinople, would survive until 1453, when it was conquered by Islamic forces. But in the west the Christian Roman Empire was no more.

The empire in the west had fallen to so-called barbarian tribes whose original homelands lay outside the Roman Empire, although many had been on the move for generations. Most of these spoke various Germanic languages. Some served as mercenary troops in the Roman Empire; others raided the rich imperial lands. Under increasing pressure, the borders of the empire could no longer withstand this and imploded. In this way the fifth and sixth centuries witnessed the break-up of the western empire and the establishment of a mosaic of barbarian successor kingdoms. Roman Britain became a patchwork of Anglo-Saxon kingdoms battling western British (Celtic) kingdoms; Gaul became the kingdoms of the Franks and the Burgundians; Spain the kingdom of the Visigoths; Italy that of the Ostrogoths and then the Lombards. And this simplifies an even more complex and shifting reality!

The survival of the faith of the cross

At first many of these tribes were pagan, worshipping the Germanic gods of northern Europe such as Woden/Odin and Thunor/Thor. But as Rome collapsed, Christianity both survived and spread its geographical reach. The barbarian tribes of the Goths and Burgundians converted to a heretical – Arian – form of Christianity, but they were later re-converted to Catholic beliefs. Along the Rhine and in northern France the pagan Franks converted to Catholic Christianity and were followed in the seventh century by the pagan kingdoms of Anglo-Saxon England. In the far west and north-west, Christianity survived unbroken from the Roman Empire among the British kingdoms. Missionaries from Britain took the faith to Ireland in the fifth century and from there missionaries returned to preach to pagan Anglo-Saxons in what is today England, and pagan Picts and Scots in what is today Scotland.

By the year 1000, Christianity had spread far across the Germanic kingdoms, and it was in this same year that Scandinavia's far-flung colony of settlers in Iceland decided to adopt Christianity (see Chapter 6).

In each of these new Christian successor kingdoms the symbol of the cross continued to be the defining feature of the newly adopted set of beliefs. Familiarity with the cross came via a number of routes. At Sutton Hoo (Suffolk, England) probable diplomatic gifts from the Eastern Roman Empire to the barbarian ruler of East Anglia included ten silver bowls, each of which was decorated with an equal-armed cross carefully inscribed into the inside of each bowl.[1] Other crosses accompanied the work of Christian missionaries. When such kingdoms converted to Christianity, much preaching took place at standing crosses before sufficient churches were built. Frankish kings minted gold coins inscribed with various forms of cross (for example, cross-on-globe, cross-on-steps, equal-armed cross), which carried on the tradition we have seen on Byzantine coins. By the eighth century many of the fine silver pennies of Offa of Mercia (in England) also carried crosses and it was a tradition that would continue far into the Middle Ages. These kings were adopting the symbols of imperial belief and rule, and the cross was a key part of that statement.[2]

In each of these new Christian successor kingdoms the symbol of the cross continued to be the defining feature of the newly adopted set of beliefs. Familiarity with the cross came via a number of routes.

Fusions and new takes on an established form

As we explore a little of the way in which the cross was presented, we can see how these newly converted Christian peoples approached it and saw it through the lens of their particular culture, so that what emerges is an intriguing fusion of the art and ideology of the Mediterranean world with that of the Germanic north and the Celtic west.

Picture 5.1
Kildalton High Cross, on Islay, Inner Hebrides. Dating from the second half of the eighth century.

Some of the most striking examples of this can be seen in the way Celtic and Germanic art combined in the cross art of Irish and Anglo-Saxon societies. On the island of Islay, the southernmost of the Scottish Inner Hebrides, can be found the Kildalton High Cross. Dating from the second half of the eighth century, it is often considered the finest surviving Celtic cross in Scotland *(Picture 5.1)*. It is a survival of Celtic Christianity that fuses Celtic and Mediterranean art styles on the cross. Elaborate curving spirals and interlace, which are also found on secular jewellery, are mixed with images of the Virgin and Child that derive from Mediterranean originals. It is part of a wider tradition, since similar artwork can be found on folio 7v of the *Book of Kells*. Other images link the cross to Bible-derived motifs of victory over sin and death: David fights a lion and Abraham is shown about to sacrifice Isaac (but God will intervene). The scene showing Cain murdering Abel (which brought judgment and condemnation) was probably meant to contrast with the death of Christ that brought blessing and life. Carved from hard local grey-green epidiorite stone, it has withstood the weathering and lichen growth that has obscured the features of crosses carved from less durable rock.

An even more dramatic mixture of artistic styles can be seen on the "Carpet Page" (due to a similarity to oriental rugs) of St Matthew's Gospel, from the manuscript known as the *Lindisfarne Gospels* *(Picture 5.2)*. Produced in Northumbria in the early eighth century, this cross is a dramatic fusion of Celtic spirals and interlaced ribbon-like animals derived from Anglo-Saxon art. This is the cross as seen through Irish and Anglo-Saxon craftspeople, hence its description as being "Hiberno-Saxon". What is intriguing is that this cross may have deliberately evoked images of

Picture 5.2
Hiberno-Saxon cross on the "Carpet Page" of St Matthew's Gospel, from the *Lindisfarne Gospels*, early eighth century. British Library, London.

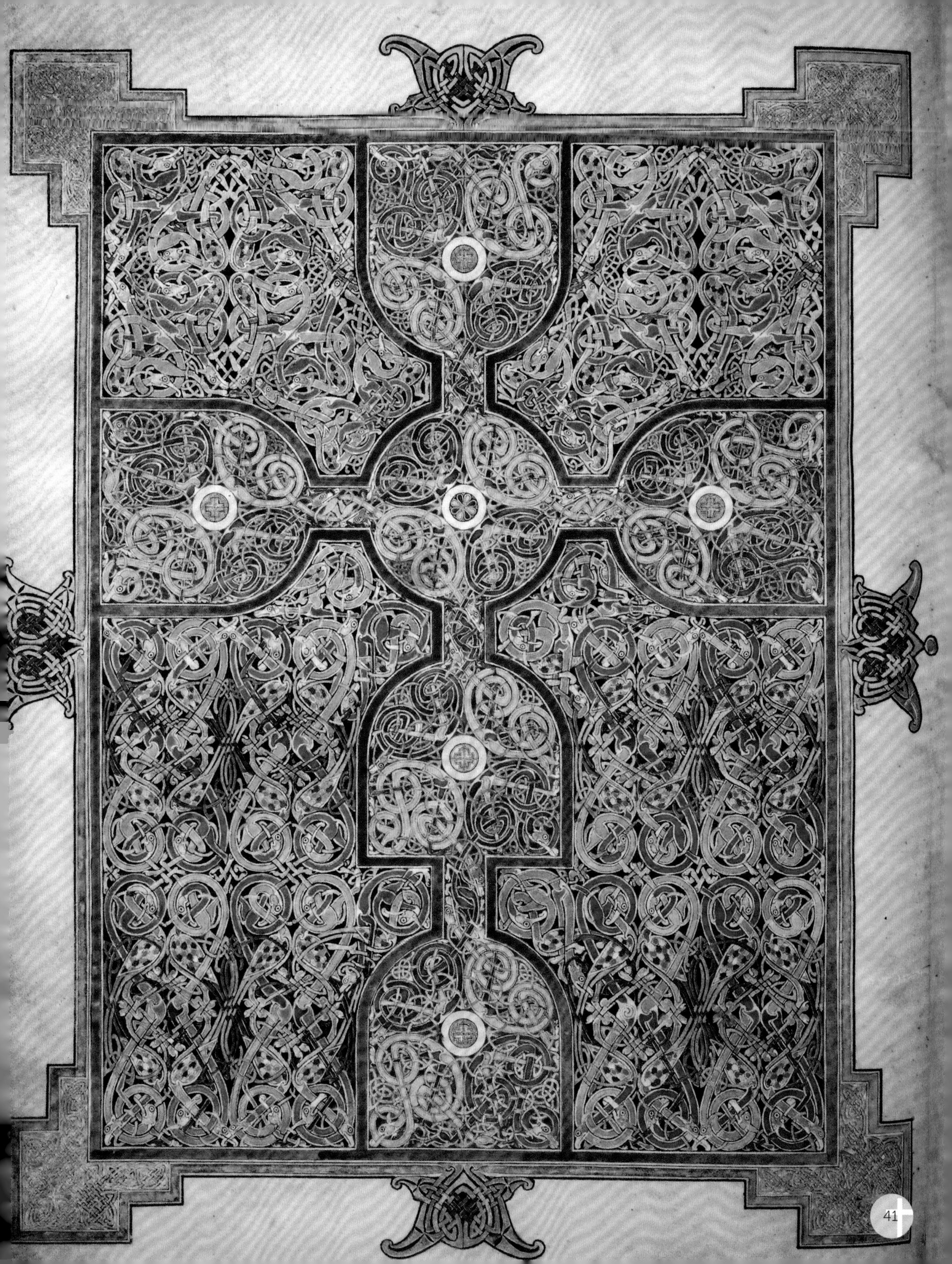

Picture 5.3
St Cuthbert's Pectoral Cross, late seventh century. Durham Cathedral.

prayer mats, which were known at the time from Coptic (Christian) Egypt and were sometimes used in Northumbria. Just as the prayer mat was part of the believer's preparation for prayer, so this cross mentally prepares the reader for meeting with God in the words of the gospel that follow. This cross is also reminiscent of the *crux gemmata* (the jewelled cross) that we met in Chapter 4.[3]

Such a cross can be seen in an Anglo-Saxon context in the St Cuthbert's Pectoral Cross, now in Durham Cathedral *(Picture 5.3)*. Constructed from gold and garnets, it was removed from the tomb of St Cuthbert (who died in 687) when the tomb was opened in 1827.

The cross as the battlefield of the warrior Christ

Christ was regarded as a warrior saviour among the barbarian successors to the Roman Empire. And while some of the descriptions used of him may be unfamiliar to modern readers, they are simply Anglo-Saxon ways of expressing kingship, sovereignty and victory over evil. An example is the poem known as *The Dream of the Rood*, in which the cross itself (the Rood) speaks of the suffering and victory of the young warrior Christ on the cross: "Then I saw, marching toward me [the cross], mankind's brave King [Christ]… Almighty God ungirded Him, eager to mount the gallows, unafraid in the sight of many: He would set free mankind."[4]

The military nature of Christ is clear from this poem. He is described as "marching", he is "unafraid", he is "eager" for battle. In another section of the poem he is described as "the great King, liege lord of the heavens…". This is a warrior noble as any Anglo-Saxon king or warrior would recognize him, and the cross is the battlefield on which this warrior Christ achieves his greatest victory. This clearly caught the Anglo-Saxon imagination, since the poem survives in whole or part on no fewer than three items. Written in the Northumbrian Old English dialect it was carved, in runes, on the eighth-century Ruthwell Cross (Dumfriesshire, Scotland). Then, written in an expanded form, it is found in a late tenth-century anthology of Anglo-Saxon prose and verse that is now known as the *Vercelli Book*. Finally, parts of it survive as a quotation on an early eleventh-century silver reliquary that was made to hold a fragment of the "True Cross" and which is now known as the Brussels Cross. This is now held in the treasury of the St Michael and St Gudula Cathedral, Brussels, Belgium. On it the Old English quotation is dramatic in its stark simplicity: "*Rod is min nama; geo ic ricne Cyning bær byfigynde, blod bestemed*" ("Rood is my name. Trembling once, I bore a powerful king, made wet with blood").[5]

As in the Byzantine Empire, the Frankish and Anglo-Saxon kings not only expressed Christ and the cross in their own terms but also linked (and enhanced) their own royal authority by association with him.

Picture 5.4

The crucifixion, from the *Sacramentary* (or *Missal*) *of Robert of Jumièges*, early eleventh century (c. 1020). Bibliothèque municipal, Rouen.

From barbarian successor states to mainline Christians

By the tenth and eleventh centuries the kingdoms that had once been the rough-and-ready successor states to the Christian late Roman Empire had come of age. Efficiently administered, cultured and sophisticated, their artwork was now part of the Christian mainstream. This can be seen in the crucifixion scene from the *Sacramentary* (or *Missal*) *of Robert of Jumièges*,[6] that dates from the early eleventh century *(Picture 5.4)*. It was probably produced at Canterbury and came into the possession of the Norman Robert of Jumièges (bishop of London, 1044–51), who then gifted it to the abbey of Jumièges in France. There it remained until 1791.

It is decorated in the "Winchester style", with its lush, even exuberant, acanthus foliage (originally derived from the Carolingian Frankish Empire across the Channel) and a colouring reminiscent of artwork from the Eastern Roman (Byzantine) Empire.[7] This particular example, with its impressionistic style, scribbled background and ornate drapery, takes inspiration from the north-eastern-French "Reims Style".[8] This style became highly influential in the development of medieval art.[9] Furthermore, it is an example of crucifixion scenes in which the emotion is embodied in the onlookers (Mary covers her face in grief and the disciple raises his hand to his sorrowful face), but Christ himself is calm and without any sign of pain (see Chapter 4). There is no blood and there are no visible nails.

But even as this stage in the representation of the cross was occurring in the successor states to Rome, something more shockingly dramatic was taking place among the Germanic peoples, who were the last to convert to Christianity. For among the Scandinavian Norse communities of the Viking Age there was a very different approach to the cross.

Chapter 6

THE CROSS AND HAMMER (VIKINGS)

In the year 1000, Thorgeir Thorkelsson, lawspeaker of Iceland, threw his pagan idols into the thundering waterfall of Goðafoss, on the river Skjálfandafljót in north-eastern Iceland. In so doing, he took part in one of the last Christian conversions of the northern Germanic peoples.

Few cultures offer us a more striking combination of indigenous culture and artistic imagery with established Christian understanding of Christ than the last of the Germanic peoples to convert to Christianity: the Vikings.

Viking figures of a bound Christ

The very first representation of the crucified Christ to be found in Viking-Age Denmark dates from the early tenth century (900–50).[1] Discovered in a field near Aunslev, East Funen, in 2016 was a figure of Christ made from fine gold threads and small filigree pellets[2] *(Picture 6.1)*. What has been called the "Aunslev Cross" is the first complete example so far discovered in Denmark. Earlier fragments from similar crosses (but made from silver) had been discovered in a silver hoard from Omø and in a burial within a waggon at Ketting, on the island of Als.[3] A similar figure and dating from the same time period (but made from gilded silver) was unearthed in 1879, at Birka, in the Swedish province of Uppland. There, in Grave 660, a wealthy woman declared her Christian faith, but in a way very recognizably Scandinavian. As in the Danish example from Aunslev, this Swedish Viking Christ is dressed in trousers, like a contemporary Viking male, and is *bound* to the cross. It is clear that the concept of nailed crucifixion had not been fully understood, or was not considered a vital part of the depiction among these early Scandinavian Christians. It is very likely that the bound Christ was a reworking of the Norse myth of the binding of Odin, who underwent this in order to gain power over runes. If so, it is a well-evidenced example of the use of existing imagery to convey a new message.

Picture 6.1
Bound crucifixion gold pendant. Found near Aunslev, East Funen, Denmark, c. 900–50. Vikingemuseet Ladby.

Picture 6.2

Jelling Stone, Denmark. Erected by King Harald Bluetooth (c. 965) in memory of his parents, King Gorm and Queen Thyra. This reconstruction shows the probable original appearance.

In a similar way, the vine-entwined crucifixion scene from the royal memorial stone at Jelling, in Denmark (dating from c. 965), also represents a bound Christ rather than one nailed to the cross. In fact, Christ stands with arms wide in crucifixion pose, but there is actually no cross. This stone was erected by Harald Bluetooth, the first Christian king of any Scandinavian kingdom, in memory of his father and mother. When originally raised it would have been dramatically painted in vivid colours *(Picture 6.2)*. Before the discovery of the silver and gold crucifixion pendants, it was thought to be the oldest crucifixion scene from Scandinavia.

Pagan images to convey the message of the cross

A number of other examples exist of pagan motifs being reinvented in order to convey the message of the cross. This can be seen most obviously in some tenth-century examples from areas of Viking settlement in the British Isles. On the Gosforth Cross, from Cumbria, the figure of the crucified Christ is accompanied by a Valkyrie-like female figure. In Viking mythology these warrior women were believed to choose the best of slain warriors to join the warband of the Viking god Odin. The presence of such a figure on the Gosforth Cross may have conveyed the idea of a warrior Christ that is reminiscent of the Anglo-Saxon poem *The Dream of the Rood* (see Chapter 5). There may even have been a conflation of the belief in a Valkyrie at the death scene of a warrior with traditional images of Mary Magdalene standing at the foot of the cross. The use of Viking myths to communicate the new Christian message also influenced other carvings on this cross. Other scenes relate to the Scandinavian myth of Ragnarok (the destruction of the gods and the end of the world): the Viking watchman god Heimdall confronts two open-jawed serpents; the wife of the trickster god Loki attempts to prevent serpent venom from dripping on him as he is being punished for crimes against fellow gods and goddesses.

When crosses appeared in Scandinavia as Christian statements of faith, they seem to have prompted a reaction from pagans who felt under threat. This reaction revealed itself in the appearance of Thor's-hammer pendants.

It is easy to conclude that these images are examples of syncretism (the mixing of different religions). If so, Christ and the message of the cross has been awkwardly bolted on to the pantheon of pagan Viking gods. In a similar way, silver pennies minted for Sihtric (Viking king of York: 921–27) – and recently found as part of a hoard at Thurcaston, near Leicester – carry a picture of a hammer of the Scandinavian god Thor and a sword on one side and a Christian cross on the other. There are even little crosses next to the sword.

However, the images on the stone crosses are probably more subtle than this. And we do not have to view these Viking examples as the naive art of first-generation converts who had not really grasped the Christian understanding of Christ and the cross. It is more likely that as the stone carvers sought to communicate this central and dramatic Christian belief, they selected carefully chosen motifs from pagan mythology in order to make the ideas more accessible to an audience of new converts. While we cannot be certain, the association with Viking ideas concerning the end of the world may have been intended to draw parallels between Christ's victory over sin, death and evil, and pre-existing ideas about conflicts with cosmic forces of destruction and suffering (represented by the open-jawed serpents and the damage caused by the deeds of Loki).

There is good reason for thinking this, because the Gosforth Cross is not unique in this respect. At Kirk Andreas, on the Isle of Man, a cross slab (known as Thorwald's Cross and dating to c. 950) depicts to one side of the cross another scene from Ragnarok. Here we see the chief god Odin, identified by the raven on his shoulder, being devoured by a terrible wolf known from Scandinavian mythology as Fenrir. It is likely that these scenes from Ragnarok were selected in order to evoke thoughts concerning the Christian concept of Judgment Day, but communicated in a traditional style. Their place on a Christian cross would be considered appropriate because, as the symbol of where salvation was achieved, the cross promised a way by which believers would survive the destruction and condemnation inherent in Judgment Day and the end of the world (the latter a belief as integral to Christianity as to pagan Scandinavians). Indeed, the fact that Ragnarok involved the destruction of the Viking gods (epitomized by Odin devoured by the wolf Fenrir) may have given it particular resonance as a reminder of the victory of Christ over them. In this way these images of a Viking Christ were carefully communicated in order to make the message of the cross understood. They were not simply naive misunderstandings or ideological compromises. Instead, they were important stages in the communication of the story of the cross to the people of the north.

Crosses and hammers

This said, there were still areas of compromise in the first generations following the conversion. The Icelandic manuscript called *Landnamabok* (*Book of Settlements* – of Iceland) says of one early settler – Helgi the Lame – that he believed in Christ but prayed to Thor before a sea journey or when in need of warrior courage. As this source comments, his faith was "very mixed".[4] Given this mixing of faiths, it is perhaps not surprising to learn that it affected the use of the cross as a symbol. When crosses appeared in Scandinavia as Christian statements of faith, they seem to have prompted a reaction from pagans who felt under threat. This reaction revealed itself in the appearance of Thor's-hammer pendants. These were worn by some pagans, it seems,

Picture 6.3

King Cnut (king of Denmark and England) and Queen Emma giving a gold cross to the church at Winchester, 1020s. From the *New Minster Liber Vitae*, British Library, London.

as a kind of "anti-cross".[5] Not only did Scandinavian pagan art begin to mimic the new representational styles, it also became more uniform,[6] as if attempting to meet the threat posed by the distinct nature of Christian iconography. This became particularly apparent in the competing area of crosses and hammers.

In Viking-Age mythology, Thor's hammer – named *Mjöllnir* – was the symbol of the god of war and weather. There was a superficial similarity between the shape of the cross and the shape of the hammer (which, when worn, resembled a *Tau Cross*[7] upside down). The size of cross pendants and hammer pendants being similar suggests they were used in similar ways. And Helgi the Lame was not the only one to mix his faith; others mixed *symbols* too. A woman buried at Thumby-Bienebek, near Hedeby in Denmark, wore a cross pendant around her neck but lay in a waggon decorated with hammers. One pendant, from western Sweden, is decorated with both crosses and hammers. A soapstone mould from Jutland, Denmark, was used to make metal crosses *and* hammers.[8]

The victory of the cross

By the year 1000 almost all the Scandinavian peoples had officially converted to Christianity. And in England it was the king of a united Danish-English Empire, Cnut (king: 1016–35), who in 1020 banned all forms of idol worship, since it had been reintroduced to Christian Anglo-Saxon England by the latest waves of Viking settlers. As a sign of how far Scandinavian rulers and their subjects had embraced Christianity, Cnut made a public statement when he placed a gold cross on the altar of New Minster, Winchester, in the 1020s *(Picture 6.3)*. In the pictured portrait, with his right hand he firmly holds the cross that he is placing on the altar, and his name (*CNVT*) is prominently displayed beside the cross. His left hand rests on his sword hilt as a statement of his warrior status, but an angel crowns him and points to Christ in majesty, seated above the cross.[9] The message of the Christian faith is explicit: the hammer has clearly given way to the cross.

Chapter 7

THE CHALLENGE OF ISLAM: CRUSADER CROSS, CRUSADER CHRIST?

The Islamic conquests in the Middle East and North Africa challenged Christianity over the central role of the cross. Those Western knights who went on crusade were described as "taking the cross". Illuminated manuscripts depicted Christ as a crusader, and the Christian response to Islamic conquests was closely associated with the cross as a symbol. Indeed, this was so pronounced that it even culminated in the capture by Muslims of what Christians described as the "True Cross" at the Battle of Hattin, in 1187.

A heavily contested symbol in a heavily contested city

Islam venerates Jesus as a prophet and as the messiah sent by God (*Allah* in Arabic). In Arabic he is described as *Isa ibn Maryam, al-Masih* (Jesus, son of Mary, the messiah). However, in stark contrast with Christian belief, the Qur'an teaches that Jesus was not in fact crucified but was taken up to heaven without such a death occurring:

> *[The People of the Book[1]] said, "We have killed the Messiah, Jesus, son of Mary, the Messenger of God." (They did not kill him, nor did they crucify him, though it was made to appear like that to them; those that disagreed about him are full of doubt, with no knowledge to follow, only supposition: they certainly did not kill him – No! God raised him up to Himself. God is almighty and wise...)[2]*

Some Muslims believe that God changed the face of Judas, Jesus' betrayer, so that he looked like Jesus. Judas was then crucified in Jesus' place; it was only made to appear that Jesus was crucified. This belief is that the cross is not a sign of the cleansing of human sin through the sacrifice and resurrection of Jesus, but a sign of divine justice: Jesus' betrayer was given the punishment he deserved for such a deed of betrayal.

This is a very different understanding of the cross compared with the belief that is central to Christianity. As we have seen, a core belief of Christianity is that Jesus was the Son of God (a belief rejected by Islam) and that, despite this divine status, he died on the cross as the means by which sinful humans can be reconciled to God the Father. The cross, for Christians, is central to how they understand the role and achievements of Jesus. It is, therefore, a major point of difference between Christianity and Islam. When some modern-day Islamists describe Christians as "people of the cross"[3] they are referring to a symbol that is a defining point of a central difference between Christianity and Islam. In the same way, the importance of Jerusalem also became heavily contested in the run-up to the crusades.

When some modern-day Islamists describe Christians as "people of the cross" they are referring to a symbol that is a defining point of a central difference between Christianity and Islam.

As early as the year 638, Jerusalem had been captured by an Islamic army; prior to that it had been a city of the Christian Byzantine Empire. Given the central place of Jerusalem within the life, death, resurrection and ascension of Christ, it is not surprising that this Jewish holy city had become a Christian holy place. Furthermore, Christians believed that it would be to Jerusalem that Christ would return in glory at his second coming, to judge the world and bring the fulfilment of God's kingdom.

However, the city was also later regarded as holy by Muslims, since they believe that Muhammad was miraculously transported from Mecca (Makkah) to Jerusalem during what is known as the "Night Flight" and, while in Jerusalem, briefly ascended into heaven. Its capture by Muslims brought a key Christian holy place under Islamic control.

The cross and the crusades

The seventh-century capture of Jerusalem by Muslims did not lead to the launching of the crusades. Indeed, for over 400 years it remained under Islamic rule, with Christian pilgrims visiting it. It was not until 1095 that the First Crusade was launched, with the aim of recapturing Jerusalem for Christendom. It succeeded in so doing in 1099, and went on to establish the Christian crusader kingdom of Jerusalem and the principalities of Edessa, Antioch and Tripoli.

The re-conquest of Edessa by Islamic forces in 1144 led to the Second Crusade, which ended in a military disaster. The eventual capture of Jerusalem by Sultan Saladin (Salah al-Din Yusuf ibn Ayubb) in 1187 triggered the Third Crusade. This was famously led by the Holy Roman Emperor Frederick Barbarossa, King Philip II of France and King Richard I – "the Lionheart" – of England. It failed to recapture Jerusalem, but by 1191 Richard had conquered the city of Acre after a lengthy siege, and had secured a narrow strip of land along the coast. Jerusalem remained under Islamic rule. The Fourth Crusade, of 1203–04, only succeeded in severely damaging the Christian Byzantine Empire when Western – Latin – forces sacked Constantinople and set up their own short-lived Latin kingdom of Constantinople, accompanied by other states in Greece. Jerusalem was briefly regained by Christians in 1229, but was finally lost to Islamic control in 1244. In 1291 the last crusader state in the Middle East ended when the city of Acre was finally taken by Islamic forces.

As early as the First Crusade, the cross – already the well-established symbol of Christianity – became the defining symbol of those going on crusade with the aim of recapturing Jerusalem. Famously, the pope called on them to "take the cross", and the symbol was worn on crusaders' surcoats and was carried on banners. Soon, knightly crusading orders – such as the Knights Templar and the Knights Hospitaller – took crosses as their symbols: the red cross of the Templars; the white cross on black of the Hospitallers. Consistent with this heraldry, Jesus was depicted leading cross-marked crusaders into battle in medieval manuscript illustrations *(Picture 7.1)*.

This only served to aggravate Islamic opposition to the Christian concept of the cross. What had started as a major theological difference regarding the death of Jesus now became symbolic of a violently contested ideological divide which centred on the cross. Given the medieval use of coats of arms, it is not surprising that the cross soon featured on many of them, as we have seen. What is perhaps more surprising is how

Picture 7.1
Christ leading crusaders with red-cross banners, from an English manuscript entitled the *Queen Mary Apocalypse*, dating from the first quarter of the fourteenth century. British Library, London.

Picture 7.2

A knightly coat of arms attributed to Jesus, including instruments of the Passion. From the fifteenth-century *Hyghalmen Roll.* English College of Arms, London.

the military conflict with Islam led to the presentation of Christ as if he were himself a crusader. One of the most striking examples of this can be found in a medieval manuscript known as the *Hyghalmen Roll (Picture 7.2)*. This invented a knightly coat of arms for Jesus. He is actually represented as a knight. His face is hidden within a great helm and the helm itself supports symbols that mirror the heraldic devices carried on knights' helmets. In the case of Christ, the symbols are a high wooden cross with nails driven into it, a three-tailed whip with metal pieces tied into the leather, and a six-branched wooden scourge. These are the symbols of Christ's suffering and death. In his right hand he holds a lance, the pennant of which depicts the

Lamb of God holding a cross standard and standing beside the chalice of the Eucharist (Holy Communion). In his left hand he raises his shield. On a blue background is pictured the Head of Christ: the medieval relic called the "Veil of Veronica" or "Veronica's Handkerchief". This was thought to bear the miraculous imprint of Christ's face, produced when Veronica gave him the cloth to wipe his face on the way to his crucifixion. Veronica was later believed to have lived in Jerusalem at the time of Christ and to have taken pity on him. In this way the cross and crucifixion had become a heraldic symbol of Christ as a crusader knight, in a striking militarization of how Christ was depicted.

The capture of the "True Cross"

The Christian veneration of pieces of the "True Cross" only intensified Islamic opposition to its use as a symbol and led to accusations of idolatry on the part of Christians; an accusation they vigorously denied.

In the early eleventh century, the holy relic of the cross held in Jerusalem was hidden by Christians to protect it and it was not revealed again until crusader knights retook the city in 1099. It became the most treasured relic of the crusader kingdom of Jerusalem and was kept in the Church of the Holy Sepulchre. It was captured by the Islamic ruler Saladin during the Battle of Hattin in 1187, in which he crushed the army of the kingdom of Jerusalem. After this it was paraded upside down on a lance through the streets of Damascus. Nothing could better illustrate how deeply the symbol divided Christians and Muslims. From there this particular relic vanished from history.

The drama of this loss is arrestingly illustrated in the account of the defeat at Hattin as recounted by the St Albans chronicler Matthew Paris (lived: 1200–59) in his *Chronica Majora* (*Major Chronicles*). This depicts the (imagined) height of the battle at Hattin, in which two crusaders – King Guy of Jerusalem and Count Raymond – grapple with Saladin himself for possession of the "True Cross". The drama of the event is clear: Saladin seizes the two arms of the cross, which are also being gripped by King Guy, who is being pulled backwards from his horse; Count Raymond leans forward in his saddle to grab the foot of the cross in a vain attempt to stop its loss. Other warriors are also engaged in the fight, and beneath the hooves of their horses can be seen the severed heads and limbs of those slain in the contest for this holy relic *(Picture 7.3)*.

fuit uel gladius interfecta. Euaserunt tamen ab
hac clade comes tripolitanus licet omnibus suis
pectus dominus reginaldus sydonis patronus atque
dominus balianus cum paucis fratribus milicie
templi. Facta est autem hec misera belli congres
sio quinto scilicet et quarto nonas iulii infra
octauas apostolorum petri et pauli. Euasit etiam ab
hac clade theodoricus magister milicie templi.

Saladin'
Guido
rex
Crux
sca

The emphasis placed on the "True Cross" during the crusades, and its place as a relic to be carried into battle, was part of the militarization of Christ and his death that accompanied the drive to recapture Jerusalem. It was one of the most controversial episodes in the story of the cross and continues to reverberate into the twenty-first century.

Picture 7.3

Saladin shown capturing the "True Cross" at the Battle of Hattin, 1187. From the *Chronica Majora*, produced at St Albans, England, c. 1240–53. Now in the Parker Library, Corpus Christi College, Cambridge.

Chapter 8

SUFFERING ON THE CROSS

By the High Middle Ages, the crucifixion was beginning to be displayed in a more realistic fashion: the figure of Jesus appeared dead on the cross, with eyes closed, bowed head and sagging body. This was first influenced by the earlier so-called Iconoclastic controversy (726–843), which occurred within the Byzantine Empire, where some influential members of the Eastern Orthodox Church challenged the veneration of images. This eventually resulted in the reinstatement of icons in Orthodox worship with a more realistic representation of the actual death of Christ on some of these, as the reality of what they portrayed became part of the defence of their use. However, though realistically dead, the Christ figure on these early crucifixes appears with an unbroken body and with no expression of pain. This selective realism was to continue in Eastern Orthodox art, but in western Europe the trajectory of realism came to include both pain and brokenness.

The crucifix emphasizing the humanity of Christ

It was significant that the duality of Christ's nature (both human and divine) had become firmly established in church doctrine, and so the Western church's approach to the image of the cross moved away from the need to show a glorified Christ, towards the depiction of his suffering humanity and identifying with Christ as part of a personal sense of redemption through the cross in the mind of the viewer.

Although this appreciation of the suffering endured on the cross had always been present in Christian theology, monastic communities also began to increasingly focus on how it was through Jesus' *suffering* that salvation was won. As St Anselm (1033–1109) put it, the "sacrifice of Christ is an offering of his perfect humanity on behalf of sinful man".[1] Because of this perfect humanity his suffering was believed to be greater than that known by any ordinary man or woman. This acted as a further stimulus to accurate portrayal of Christ's suffering. This portrayal of the pain experienced by Jesus was, therefore, stimulated by an increased emphasis on the Christian belief in the incarnation: God becoming truly man. Graphic wounds displayed the taking on of human weakness as Christ, in his humanness, drew humanity back to God.

In the thirteenth century, the production of devotional images by communities of monks and friars led to the widespread dissemination of crucifixes with these graphic images. St Francis of Assisi (1181–1226), who had a marked and deeply personal devotion to the crucified Christ, was influential in this movement. The Franciscans encouraged private devotional images of the Passion in order to increase the reverence of believers' responses. Indeed, so passionate was St Francis's devotion to the suffering Christ that it was claimed he received the five "stigmata wounds" on his own body as a visual sign of his identification with Christ.

Picture 8.1
Crucifix, by Cimabue (also known as Cenni di Pepo), c. 1265. Museo di Santa Croce, Florence.

In this way, meditational devotion in the thirteenth century became more intense as it coincided with more realistic and emotionally charged depictions of Christ's anguish and as it encouraged individual empathy with him. More and more artists exposed the human emotions and bodily weakness of Christ visually. The attempts at physical accuracy in such paintings as Cimabue's *Crucifix*, c. 1265 *(Picture 8.1)* were intended to aid a spiritual understanding of the event portrayed. Consequently, this period represented a time of growing emphasis on the need to show first-century events on the cross as they really occurred, and as identified by the witness of the New Testament.

As the movement emphasizing a more empathetic engagement with Christ as a man crucified for

Picture 8.2
The *Isenheim Altarpiece*, 1512–16, by Matthias Grünewald. Unterlinden Museum, Colmar, Alsace.

humanity gained strength in the fourteenth century, traumatic social events also influenced the religious mentality of European Christendom. The catastrophic effects of the Black Death, and the resulting exposure of the frailty of human life, accelerated the growing emphasis upon a human and suffering Christ. And it continued to influence artwork long after the first fourteenth-century outbreaks of plague. The *Isenheim Altarpiece (Picture 8.2)*, painted between 1512 and 1516 by Matthias Grünewald, depicts the crucified Christ as a plague victim covered in sores. Grünewald painted the altarpiece for the Monastery of St Anthony in Isenheim, now in north-eastern France, which specialized in caring for victims of the plague and other skin diseases. The believers' own sufferings were reflected in the image of Christ's death on the cross, the suffering of Christ on the cross encompassing the suffering of his followers.

The cross and the flagellants

The troubled fourteenth century was also an era of penitential enthusiasm. The so-called Brethren of the Common Life (a lay community founded in Flanders) took part in bloodletting processions as they identified with a Christ who was wounded, bloodied and mutilated. But in a step beyond this, these practitioners of mortification would whip their own flesh as both a demonstration of their piety and penance, and in an attempt to satisfy God's wrath, and halt what was understood to be divine judgment on their plague-ridden communities.[2] The flagellants at Doornik (Tournai) in 1349 *(Picture 8.3)* are portrayed carrying the crucifix at the head of their march as they replicate its suffering in their own bodies.

For the majority of believers, though (and flagellants always constituted a tiny minority), this personal insight into what Christ experienced was gained through art. In this experience the believer could both meditate on Christ's suffering and – as they worshipped – hope to move towards personal holiness without imitating the self-harm practised by the flagellants. This attention to the five wounds of crucifixion marked on Christ's body became one of the principal devotions of the later Middle Ages.

Taken together, this change in appearance of the cross in art illustrated an awakening of emotional identification that went well beyond the physical imitation embodied in flagellant behaviour. Devotion to the crucified Christ had come to involve emotional reactions to the imagery, engaging the imagination to stimulate identification with the suffering Christ – and also thinking beyond oneself to the suffering of the world. A writer known as Pseudo-Bede stated in 1300 that the believer "must feel grief as if the Lord were suffering before their very eyes".[3] From such graphic images extended an urgent call to personally respond to such a display of divine love.

The lay movements originating in Flanders therefore urged a stronger emotional engagement on the part of the non-clerical faithful in particular, as the man on the cross was understood as "one of us", a suffering human being. There had been an evolution of faith alongside the realistic artistic progression: people's

Picture 8.3
Flagellants in the Netherlands town of Doornik (Tournai). A miniature from the *Chronicle of Aegidius Li Muisis*, 1349. Bibliothèque Royale, Brussels.

experiences of contemporary suffering had impacted on how they both understood and related to the suffering Christ.

The crucifix and "Man of Sorrows" images

As well as crucifix images, "Man of Sorrows" images also emerged by the fifteenth century, such as Geertgen van Haarlem's Flemish depiction *(Picture 8.4)*, c. 1485–95. These often portrayed the prelude to crucifixion. The tears, bloody body and direct, distressed gaze all served to pinpoint human suffering as the viewer was encouraged to seek consolation and identification with Christ, a fellow human being. The painter here used all artistic means at his disposal to encourage feelings of repentance in the viewer. These images consciously echoed Isaiah 53:3, "He was despised and rejected by men; a man of sorrows and acquainted with grief; and as one from whom men hide their faces he was despised, and we esteemed him not."[4] The sympathy denied to Christ at the time of his death was compensated for by the later sympathy of

Picture 8.4
Geertgen van Haarlem's *Man of Sorrows*, c. 1485–95. Museum Catharijneconvent, Utrecht.

the believer. Furthermore, through reflection on the "Man of Sorrows", the observer was encouraged to reflect upon their own sin that caused such pain to the innocent, and by extension this also encouraged identification with all who suffer. This then demonstrated a sense of gratitude for the suffering of Christ, awareness of and remorse for human sin that led to such suffering, and realization of the salvation now available to humankind because of such an act. An appeal to empathy and compassion on the part of the believer was intended to remove the barrier between people and Christ. As one twentieth-century observer of medieval art put it, "the image of a God who suffered along with them was more psychologically appealing than the theological notion of glory".[5] A Christ who shared in universal human suffering invited people to share in his attitude and in his work of redemption. A form of sculpture (called pieta) depicted the Virgin Mary cradling the dead body of Jesus. These developed in Germany from about 1300 and from there spread across Europe.

The crucifix of victory and suffering

It appears that images of both victory and suffering existed alongside each other for some centuries, demonstrating that there was not a simple, rapid change from earlier majestic images to suffering images. Yet, for the most part, later medieval art is dominated by crucifixes showing graphic images of suffering, illustrating a new intensity of affliction, physically and emotionally. Consequently, there was clearly a gradual process of development from an emphasis on Christ's imperial grandeur, divine omnipotence and heavenly nature to a contemplation of his wounded, dying human body as the key to salvation. This latter image of Christ, which was well established by the fourteenth century, was to prevail and remain through to the twenty-first century. This movement to a more realistic, even bloody, representation – emphasizing Christ's human suffering – contrasts with previous majestic depictions of the cross.

Initially, a reworking of theology drove the progression but, at its climax, individual devotional meditation – accelerated by social crisis – drove the development. This involved more than just an artistic evolution of the image itself; it also reflected significant changes in understanding about the crucifixion event and relating to the crucified Christ. It was a significant chapter in the story of the cross

Chapter 9

THE CROSS IN AFRICA

As Christianity spread throughout Africa before the impact and restrictions imposed by the European missionaries in the nineteenth century, African history, heritage, customs and culture inspired the way in which the cross was depicted. These interpretations and depictions reflect the way in which the cross resonated with contrasting cultures in this huge continent.

Ethiopian processional crosses

Throughout Ethiopia's history, crosses have been central to the country's religious, cultural and social life, being the most significant and embellished symbol in Ethiopian art. The importance of the cross lies in its consecration by the death and blood of the crucified Christ. Consequently, it is seen as a triumphant emblem and its power offers protection. Crosses are therefore often visible in public places and in the home.

Ethiopian crosses have a distinctive African rather than European Latin look, because Christianity was not brought to Ethiopia by European missionaries, unlike many other African countries in much later periods of history. Instead, King Ezana II, ruler of Aksum or Axum (in modern-day Eritrea and Tigray regions of Ethiopia), was converted to Christianity in the fourth century by Frumentius of Tyre, and the country has embraced a form of Orthodox Christianity as their religion ever since.[1] Additionally, the Ethiopian Orthodox Church has been separated from more mainstream Christian iconography due to the spread of Islam in northern Africa and the Middle East. Also, as a result of avoiding nineteenth-century European colonialism, Ethiopia has continued to produce its own distinctive crosses. The Italian conquest in the 1930s was rapidly reversed by later Italian defeats at the hands of British Empire troops in the Second World War.

The first crosses to appear in Ethiopia were crosses on (mainly gold or silver) Aksumite coins, from the fourth century (see Chapter 3). One type of Ethiopian cross, and an important form of Ethiopian art, is the processional cross; these are often made out of metal or wood and plated (originally) with gold or silver. These pieces are usually very intricately decorated with numerous crosses included within the design; the elaborate designs are said to symbolize the richness of the hearts of the Ethiopian people.

However, these designs do not usually have an image of the crucified Christ on them. Only those crosses that were influenced later by Western iconography appear with the figure of the crucified Jesus. The Ethiopian crosses are very much crosses of resurrection. The metal heads of these processional crosses were fixed onto a long wooden staff, to be carried in religious processions and during services. As holy representations of the crucified and resurrected Jesus, the cross would be dressed with colourful cloths for ceremonial occasions and festivals.

Picture 9.1 shows a rare and early bronze Ethiopian processional cross from the twelfth or thirteenth century. Within the pear-shaped frame are two central crosses. There is a similar version of this cross in Addis Ababa, but with a crucified Christ on one of the crosses. On the version illustrated here, the pear shape appears to be a type of *mandorla* (an almond-shaped halo which, unlike the halo, encircles the whole body). It represents the

Picture 9.1
Ethiopian processional cross, dating from the twelth–thirteenth century, The Walters Art Museum, Baltimore, USA.

holiness of Jesus and is a way of exalting the crucified Christ. As well as processional crosses, it was not uncommon for smaller crosses to be worn as jewellery.

From Ethiopia, this African-derived form of the cross spread into other areas of sub-Saharan Africa. However, in other parts of Africa south of the Sahara other forms of indigenous crosses developed that also reflected African traditions but drew on very different traditional concepts.

The crosses of the kingdom of Kongo

This kingdom lay in what is now the northern part of Angola, the Republic of the Congo, the western part of the Democratic Republic of the Congo, and the southern part of Gabon. From around 1390 until 1891 this central African kingdom largely succeeded in defending its independence against Western colonial expansion. In 1891 it came under Portuguese domination and was absorbed into the neighbouring Portuguese colony of Angola.

After Ethiopia, with its sub-Saharan connections, the second great contact between Africa and Christianity (in this case Roman Catholicism) occurred with Christianity's introduction to central Africa, after the year 1483, with the arrival of the Portuguese along the coast of West Africa and their interaction with the Kongo kingdom. This led to the conversion of a local king (called by the Portuguese King Alfonso I, who ruled from 1509 to 1542), along with many of his people.[2]

The rulers of the Kongo kingdom then used Christianity as a way of developing political relations and increasing trade with European powers. This also strengthened their position in relationships with other African tribal groups.

Picture 9.2
Seventeenth-century copper alloy crucifix from the Democratic Republic of the Congo, National Museum of African Art, Smithsonian Institution, Washington DC, USA.

However, before the spread of Christianity to the Kongo kingdom, the cruciform shape already had great cosmological meaning as a *dikenga dia Kongo* or cosmogram: a representation of this world meeting the spirit world. It was often depicted as a cross within a circle.[3] The introduction of Christianity did not result in the replacement of this long-standing cosmological symbolic tradition or of local belief systems. Rather, it led to existing cross-related ideas being expressed through the adaption of the newly arrived Christian crosses. In the late fifteenth century, when Portuguese missionaries gave the Kongo rulers crucifixes as official gifts, these images became part of indigenous customs and art alongside ancestral rituals and were used as leadership regalia. In this way the crucifix images were adapted

by local artists as symbols of power and status. Consequently, these crosses became detached from any Christian context, losing contact with Christian iconography. In Kongo, crucifixes departed from Christian Christology and theological interpretations of salvation.

After the influence of early missionary activity declined in the kingdom of Kongo in the 1750s (and before Christianity was reintroduced in the nineteenth century), Kongolese artists continued making crucifixes, on which the image of Christ had African features. This was also the case with other indigenous crosses *(Picture 9.3)*. However, in Kongo the influence of local traditions often led to startling artistic developments. The seventeenth-century figure of Christ without the cross *(Picture 9.2)* illustrates African physical features and also represents Christ as being both male and female since, in Kongo, God as a perfect being comprised both male and female.[4] In this way the Christian cross was used as a vehicle for the transmission of indigenous concepts about the nature of divinity.

Picture 9.3

African cross from the Kongo culture, Congo or Angola, dating from the early seventeenth century, The Brooklyn Museum, New York, USA.

Chapter 10

CRUCIFIX OR EMPTY CROSS?

THE REFORMATION AND COUNTER-REFORMATION

Why did the sixteenth century see the appearance of empty crosses where once crucifixes that carried the body of Christ had predominated? The answer is that, increasingly, the way people saw the cross changed as Europe divided between Protestants and Catholics. Then, faced with Protestant challenges, the Catholic Church reached back into older images of the cross to reassert itself. In the Baroque churches of southern Germany, and in Spain and Italy, a revival of elaborate crucifixes and crucifixion scenes signalled this fightback.

The disintegration of Catholic Europe

In the sixteenth century the established Roman Catholic Church in Europe fractured. Critics within that church accused its leaders of corruption and vice, entanglements in politics in which the leaders of the church seemed no different from other unscrupulous rulers, raising money by the sale of "indulgences" that claimed to offer forgiveness of sins or reduction of eternal punishment in return for cash, and a trade in relics that often included fraud and even theft. But most critically, those who criticized the established church accused it of allowing layers of church tradition to smother or obscure the ideas and practices of the early church as revealed in the New Testament; and of obstructing ordinary believers from reading and studying the Bible in their everyday languages.

When Martin Luther (1483–1546) nailed his *Ninety-five Theses* to the door of the castle church at Wittenberg, in Saxony, Germany, he was not the first to demand reform. Neither was he unique in his condemnation of indulgences and of beliefs without scriptural support. But his growing conviction that salvation came only through faith in Christ and therefore a personal relationship with him as Saviour, while not unique to Luther, was to prove explosive within a church where popes and clergy, saints and the Virgin Mary had come to be seen as intermediaries between the believer and God. Where Luther stood out was in the combination of his dogged determination and a wider political mood among a number of rulers who were sympathetic to the idea of restricting the influence of the pope in their nations.

A new world was coming to birth. Catholic Europe was fracturing as those who were protesting (soon to be termed "Protestants") broke away from the control of the pope. Other Protestant thinkers in this accelerating situation of change included John Knox (c. 1514–72) in Scotland, and Huldreich Zwingli (1484–1531) and John Calvin (1509–64) in Switzerland. It was a "Reformation" of Christendom. Others with a more revolutionary agenda of social change would also take up these new ideas and they would take them in directions that Luther had never dreamed of. Radical Anabaptists would threaten the religious and social assumptions of their day. Some Anabaptists did this by preaching peaceful doctrines that challenged the contemporary order, others by bloody revolution that attacked the status quo and sought to build a "New Jerusalem" on earth.

Falling out over the cross

Protestants often criticized Catholics for what they considered to be over-elaborate ceremonies, veneration of statues and relics, and for believing these capable of working miracles. As a reaction to these perceived errors, many Protestants attempted to strip from churches and community practices anything that was not directly promoted in Scripture. There was, though, no uniformity in this. Luther and his followers tended to allow practices if they felt these were not condemned by Scripture. On the other hand, Calvin and Swiss Protestants tended to ban anything not specifically promoted in the New Testament. This latter approach tended towards austerity and collided with centuries of Catholic Christian art and activities.

As we have seen (in Chapter 8) the late medieval church put great emphasis on the suffering of Christ. By the sixteenth century this revealed itself in realistic and arresting art that emphasized the suffering of Jesus in the crucifixion.[1] An anonymous follower of the artist Hieronymus Bosch depicted the lonely isolation of Christ among his tormentors. *(Picture 10.1)*. Protestants could accept this, but not the way it translated into images that so excited the emotion of the believer that they became an object of veneration. This posed a problem for the traditional Catholic crucifix. Carrying the body of Christ, these were often treated as if they were in some way an encounter with Christ himself.[2] But where Catholics saw deep empathy in these responses, enthusiastic Protestants saw the veneration of an idol.

Among the most zealous Protestant communities these crucifixes became the object of shocking attacks. In 1523, at Pirna, Germany, it is recorded that a man spat on the crucifix. At Ulm, Germany, in 1534, a man defecated into the mouth of Jesus on the crucifix. Other crucifixes were smashed or torn apart, or the image of Jesus was beheaded. Still others were mocked by being carried in carnivals as objects of derision.[3] What motivated these shocking attacks was a rejection of the Catholic Church's promotion of these objects as "idols". In the same way the Protestant rejection of the Catholic belief in the "Real Presence" (bread and wine becoming the body and blood of Christ in the celebration of the Mass) soon led to attacks on crucifixes. This was because, in Catholic practices, these were often closely associated with the Mass, even down to the belief that some crucifixes actually bled in imitation of Christ's wounds. Such ideas were found in local folklore as well as in official Catholic claims. Opposition to such ideas was clear from an attack on a crucifix at Basel, Switzerland, in 1529. Having paraded it from the cathedral to the market place, those responsible taunted it with the words, "If you are God, help yourself; if you are man, then bleed!"[4] The crucifix did neither and was destroyed. In a related example, a manuscript illustrating objects associated with the crucifixion – now held in the Bodleian Library, Oxford – was printed in about 1500 for a Catholic believer and was later pasted into a prayer book, but with the original Catholic devotion crossed out by an English Protestant *(Picture 10.2)*. The French Calvinist Theodore Beza (1519–1605) complained in 1587 that there was no image "that the Papists have misused more severely than the crucifix".[5] It comes as no surprise to discover that he lived most of his life in the strict Calvinist environment of Geneva, Switzerland.

Picture 10.1
Christ Carrying The Cross, attributed to a follower of Hieronymus Bosch (painted between 1500 and 1535). Museum of Fine Arts, Ghent.

Those responsible for these actions would not have seen them as attacks on the cross itself but instead as attacks on what they considered errors and blasphemy. Nevertheless, the actions were extreme. However, Lutheran Protestants did not emulate the more extreme Swiss Protestants, since Lutherans usually exempted crucifixes from the ban on images appearing in churches and Luther emphasized Christ's death as the sole way by which a believer could achieve salvation. He even found on one occasion that pieces of a broken crucifix had been scattered by more extreme Protestants about a pulpit from which he was due to preach. They were determined to strip the figure of Christ from the cross. Indeed, it was reported from Berlin that when enthusiastic Calvinists tore down and smashed the crucifix that had hung in the richly decorated cathedral in 1613, it was Lutherans who wept and complained "that the likeness of our God was treated with so little mercy".[6] The bare cross was emerging in a number of communities as a distinctive Protestant alternative to the Catholic crucifix.

Picture 10.2
Catholic woodcut of *Image of Pity*, c. 1500 (later pasted into a prayer book by a Protestant, but with the inscription crossed out). Bodleian Library, Oxford.

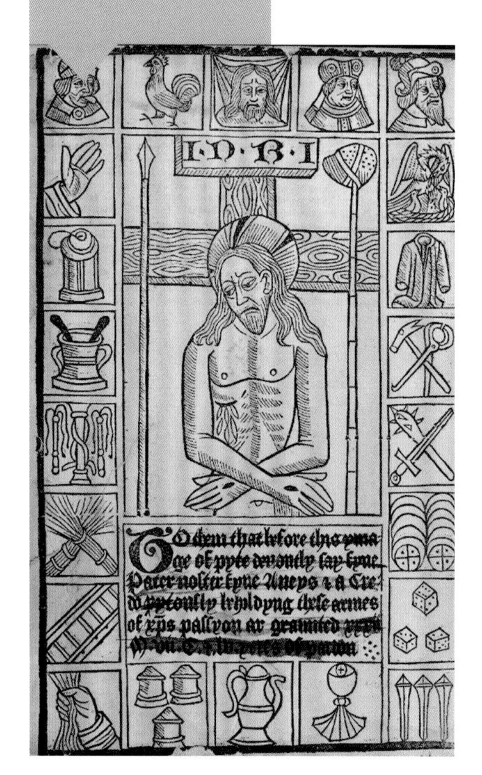

Action – and reaction – in defence of the crucifix

As Protestant ideas became entrenched in a number of states, Catholic reactions to this challenge sought to defend and legitimize the very ideas that Protestants objected to. This Counter-Reformation began with the Council of Trent (1545–63) and ended at the close of the Thirty Years' War (1648). By this time, the Protestant tide had been reversed in a number of states, although large areas of Europe remained Protestant. In the Catholic areas a resurgence of Catholic art and practice occurred.[7]

This Catholic resurgence revealed itself in depictions of the cross. This often involved a portrayal of passionate devotion to the crucified Christ and celebrations of Catholic saints whose devotion, it was believed, had caused them to be blessed by receiving the stigmata: the marks of crucifixion on their own bodies. In this way the Catholic Spanish Baroque painter Francisco Ribalta (1565–1628), in a painting of around 1620, depicted the thirteenth-century St Francis of Assisi as if he had actually been present at Christ's death *(Picture 10.3)*.

Picture 10.3

Saint Francis Embracing the Crucified Christ, by Francisco Ribalta, c. 1620. Museo de Bellas Artes, Valencia.

Picture 10.4
The Stigmatisation of St Catherine of Siena, by Rutilio Manetti, c. 1630. Now in a private collection.

A similar depiction of a stigmatic is found in a painting by the proto-Baroque Italian artist Rutilio Manetti (1571–1639). In his *The Stigmatisation of St Catherine of Siena*, c. 1630, we can see rays of light emanating from the crucifix on the altar as the fourteenth-century saint receives the stigmata on her body *(Picture 10.4)*.

In the Baroque churches of Catholic southern Europe this revived confidence was demonstrated in elaborate highly decorated churches with huge crucifixes carrying realistic depictions of Christ. These stood in stark contrast to the plain crosses found in Protestant Scandinavia,

Switzerland, England and Scotland. Even the slightly more elaborate Lutheran churches of northern Germany (where crucifixion scenes and crucifixes could still be found in churches) paled in comparison with the gilt and ornamentation of those in Catholic southern Europe. And in eastern and south-eastern Europe the Orthodox Church – untouched by the Protestant Reformation – continued in its tradition of elaborate imagery and rituals, which included elaborately jewelled crosses, such as the Serbian Orthodox cross (1630–1700), now displayed in the Victoria and Albert Museum, London *(Picture 10.5)*. Its splendour contrasts with the simplicity that became the hallmark of so many crosses in northern and western Europe, and which would be communicated by Protestant missionaries across the globe in the eighteenth and nineteenth centuries.

Picture 10.5
Serbian Orthodox cross, 1630–1700. Victoria and Albert Museum, London.

Chapter 11

NEW WORLD – NEW CROSS?

As Catholic missionaries expanded the Christian faith across South and Central America in the sixteenth and seventeenth centuries, the depictions of the cross mixed with indigenous cultures to produce a very distinct take on the cross and its significance. This also shaped developments in the Spanish-influenced regions of what is now the south-western USA and California. Other conflations of European Christian influence and Native American tradition occurred in North America.

"Black Christs" in Central America and Mexico

The earliest and most famous *Cristo Negro* or "Black Christ" of Central America and Mexico was a crucifix image of Christ in the Guatemalan town of Esquipulas, near the Honduran and El Salvadoran border *(Picture 11.1)*. In 1594 this image was sculpted from wood which, over time, blackened and gained a reputation for having miraculous powers. By 1737, various miracles had been claimed associated with this image and a sanctuary was built, which still exists today. This led to veneration of the crucifix and today over a million people visit the sanctuary every year; the *Cristo Negro de Esquipulas* is so popular that it has become known as the "Central American Capital of Faith".

Furthermore, this crucifix inspired other "Black Christ" sculptures in Mexico, such as that at Chalma, which tradition says miraculously replaced the idol of the god Oxtoteotl in 1537, and that at Otatitlán, traditionally discovered at the foot of a tree; and also the seventeenth-century image in Portobelo, Panama, traditionally washed ashore. By the end of the eighteenth century and continuing into the nineteenth, this form of image was replicated throughout Central America. Festivals were created and dedicated to them, and they remain a key feature of community life in many areas.[1] There is a possibility that these images originally acted as a replacement for the deity Yacatecuhtli, who was also represented as black.

Picture 11.1

Cristo Negro de Esquipulas, made in 1594 by Quirio Cataño, installed in the church in 1595. Cathedral Basilica of Esquipulas, in Esquipulas, Guatemala.

Other continuities

The Catholic Spanish brought a devotion to the cross that accompanied their destruction of the Mayan civilization across a region comprising south-eastern Mexico, Guatemala, Belize and the western parts of Honduras and El Salvador. In combating Mayan traditional beliefs, the Spanish leader Cortés smashed idols but placed crosses in churches and encouraged making the sign of the cross and wearing crosses. The Maya adopted this practice readily, as their religious iconography already had a cross-shape within it. Given Christ's sacrifice on the cross the Maya considered that this imbued the symbol with great protective power. But this also involved terrible distortions of use of the cross that horrified the Spaniards. Maya actually crucified children, "whose hands were nailed or tied to the cross and whose hearts were torn out". Sometimes the words "Jesus Christ" were written on the sacrificed body as a way of further enhancing the protective power of the sacrifice. Pigs and dogs were sometimes nailed to crosses.[2] In these ways, some Maya attempted to co-opt the cross into an existing tradition of both child and animal sacrifice – hoping to harness the power of the symbol and of Christ without abandoning pagan practices. The cross was also considered a symbol of the god Quetzalcoatl (in whose arms were birds and plants) by the Maya. In this way the cross became associated with the Tree of Life.

In the Andes, *cruces del camino* (roadside crosses) may have continued a pre-Christian tradition of using such symbols as waymarkers and even indicators of wind direction. In northern New Mexico, USA, a form called the *descansos* (way of rest) marked where a traveller had died.[3]

Mexican "miracle crosses"

In Mexican culture, converts to Catholicism developed the *milagro* (miracle) cross on which objects in the shape of arms, legs, praying people, farm animals and a range of other subjects were nailed or pinned. The *milagros* were left as thanks for an answered prayer. Another form of cross seen in Mexico and other parts of Latin America is the roof cross placed on the ridgepole at a roof-raising, for protection of the building. Another form of cross that derives some of its appearance from pre-Christian traditions is the Yalalag cross of the Oaxaca region of Mexico, which takes the form of a central cross from which three smaller crosses are hung.[4] In neighbouring Choapan the design more usually includes a head of Christ and *Arma Christi*: images from Christ's Passion *(Picture 11.2)*.

Picture 11.2

Mexican cross with symbols of Christ's Passion.

The Mexican Day of the Dead

The cross also appears in Mexico on Day of the Dead altars. The Day of the Dead is on 2 November, but celebrations can start from 31 October. It is uniquely Mexican, with its origins in ancestor veneration; however, due to Catholic influence, the Day of the Dead celebrations take place on All Saints' and All Souls' Day. The day remembers and honours the spirits of deceased family members and loved ones, and it is believed that their spirits will return to this world to join the celebrations. The festival combines Catholicism with ancient Aztec traditions.

An important symbol of the Day of the Dead festival is an altar that honours the deceased (an *ofrenda*). There are many elements that make up an *ofrenda* taken from indigenous Mexican and also Catholic traditions *(Picture 11.3)*. One of these elements is a cross, added by Spanish missionaries with the purpose of Christianizing existing practices. The cross is usually placed next to a picture of the dead person being remembered. There may also be a small salt cross on the altar, which is believed to purify the spirits; an ash cross on the altar is thought to help the spirits of the deceased escape purgatory. Crucifixes or crosses on top of the *ofrenda* demonstrate that neither the altar nor the deceased is to be worshipped, and emphasizes that those who are remembering the dead are Christians.

Picture 11.3
Mexican *ofrenda* (offering altar) for *Día de Muertos* (Day of the Dead).

Native American crosses of North America

In a number of Amerindian cultures, the cross was already used to represent the sun, the morning star and the four directions. In the Amazon, the tribes of the Shipibo and Canela-Quichua, for example, employed cross decorations on their painted skirts and pottery.

Similarly, northern Native Americans were open to the use of the cross due to existing traditions in their cultures *(Picture 11.4)*. For example, there is evidence that the cross symbol was important to Native Americans of the Mississippian culture of the "Mound Builders", between 1000 and 1550. The cross shape probably revealed the cosmological view of the Mound Builders: the division of the universe between the Underworld, the Middleworld (which is Earth) and the Upper world (which is heaven). The cross shape was also popular due to its simplicity: it was easy to draw on raw materials such as rock, stone, wood, shell and animal hides.[5]

It was used by a large number of Native American tribes from the plains to California. In Santa Barbara, ancient rock paintings combine cross and circle symbols. These paintings were created by the Chumash people of southern California, who used the cross to represent both religious and astronomical beliefs. Furthermore, the Solar or Cosmic Cross, which is a cross inside a circle, represents the world, as the four lines indicate the compass points. A circle within each segment of the Cosmic Cross represents one of the four elements or the key forces that originated from the Creator: fire, water, air and earth. These circles may also have signified the first four human tribes that appeared to keep the world in order. The cross here is linked to cosmological harmony.[6]

These, and other traditions, meant that European crosses were readily accepted into Native American dress and culture, even when this did not accompany Christian conversion, because it was already a part of indigenous iconography.

Picture 11.4
Nineteenth-century Cheyenne warrior wearing a cross pendant.

Chapter 12

THE CROSS IN THE AGE OF IMPERIALISM AND INDUSTRIALIZATION

Western Christian missionaries in the nineteenth century carried a very European idea of Christianity and the cross across the globe. Over time this was challenged by new converts, who borrowed from their own cultures (see Chapter 9), but this Western outlook was still influential in forming many non-European views of the cross. At the same time, industrial expansion was dramatically changing Western societies themselves and this too was reflected in portrayals of the cross.

Picture 12.1
White Christ in a European representation, nineteenth century.

White Jesus... European cross?

The growth of European empires in the eighteenth and nineteenth centuries led to the expansion of Christian missionary activity across huge areas of Africa and Asia. It is perhaps to be expected that these missionaries conveyed a very European view of Christ and therefore a very European conceptualization of the cross. The major colonial powers of the nineteenth century were Britain, France and the Netherlands, and behind them in terms of scale the Belgians and the Germans. All had a centuries-old Christian artistic tradition that stretched back into the Middle Ages and earlier. It was this that was carried to their colonies. In this they continued a tradition of transplanting Christian ideas that had earlier been pioneered by the Spanish and the Portuguese in Central and South America, and by the British, to some extent, on the eastern coast of North America.

For many converts in European empires their view of Christ and the cross was a very European view of a "White Jesus" *(Picture 12.1)*. It built on centuries of European visual traditions but made little use of local artistic conventions and was not intended to portray Christ in a way that represented indigenous peoples.

Such an approach is easily described as a "White Jesus" and a "European cross". As such it sets Christian evangelism within the wider sphere of an imperial project that aimed to bring indigenous populations under white rule and force their cultures into line with that of the imperial power. Not surprisingly, such missionaries have been categorized as "exemplary colonialist indoctrinators trampling over every cultural difference they happened to encounter".[1] But this is too negative and too simplistic. The matter was more complex. For a start, the modern anthropologists who have castigated earlier missionaries were themselves not culturally neutral and had their own agendas and impact on indigenous peoples. Furthermore, missionaries learned from – as well as influenced – indigenous cultures. It was missionary work that promoted and systematized many indigenous languages, which often then stimulated both indigenous religious expressions and secular literature. And missionaries promoted aspects of modernity that were beneficial (healthcare, scientific education) alongside those that were controversial ("acceptable" dress codes, gender relations, working practices, Western art forms).[2] It should also be remembered that the missionaries who accompanied the imperial projects were often not the first to interact with that culture. China, for example, experienced three periods of Christian missionary activity before that which occurred in the period of Western imperial expansion.[3] And in Africa, Islam too had a history of conquest that was frequently connected with the spread of Islamic religion. Tensions between Islam and Christianity in Africa predated nineteenth-century colonialism and the intense Christian missionary activity.[4]

Furthermore, in Africa (Chapter 9) and the Americas (Chapter 11) communication went both ways. In Africa there were indigenous Christian traditions that predated colonialism and there, as in the Americas, indigenous peoples soon made their own contributions to how the Christian faith and the cross should be visualized. "Adaption and coexistence was more the norm and, in many instances, African forms of Christianity emerged that would later serve as an important ideology in mobilizing resistance to European colonialism."[5] This is something we will return to in Chapter 16.

The crucifixion and industrial landscapes

Even as Europe was imposing itself on the world due to its industrial development, that very industrial change was having a huge impact on the home societies. Here the industrial revolution brought great suffering, pollution and landscape transformation alongside its eventual positive impact on European living standards. But in the bleak world of the industrial city,

Picture 12.2
Crucifixion Wigan, by Theodore Major, c. 1950. Wigan Arts and Heritage Service, Wigan.

something of the sufferings and trials of working men and women could be seen reflected in the suffering of Christ, and this in turn influenced how that suffering might be portrayed in the context of industrial society.

Theodore Major (1908–99) was born in Wigan, Lancashire, UK, and studied at Wigan Art School from 1927 to 1932. He later taught there between 1930 and 1950. In about 1950, he and his wife settled in Appley Bridge, near Wigan, and this remained their home for the rest of their lives. He was a contemporary of L. S. Lowry and, like Lowry, Major's paintings were deeply influenced by the industrial cityscapes of Lancashire. Grim and grimy Wigan streets and bleak factories appear again and again in his work.

Nowhere is this more dramatically seen than in his arresting painting entitled *Crucifixion Wigan (Picture 12.2)*, in which Christ is portrayed crucified on a telegraph pole. Although painted in 1950, it nevertheless spoke to an industrial world that was the product of the previous century, combined with the economic problems of the twentieth century. The starkness of the limited palette of colours used evokes a grim landscape of polluted northern industrial towns. The light behind the crucified figure evokes moonlight rather than sunlight and only adds to the starkness of the scene. The event seems more of the night than of the day. Pedestrians with hunched backs and bowed heads go about their business, unaware of the man crucified high above them. In the background, rows of streets, telegraph poles and industrial chimneys stretch away into the distance.

Picture 12.3

Alternative version of *Crucifixion Wigan*, by Theodore Major, c. 1950. Gateway Gallery, Hale, Cheshire.

In another – and similar – painting *(Picture 12.3)*, Major depicted a man standing on a long ladder raised against the left arm of the cross. This suggests preparation for the deposition of the body of Christ from the cross – a genre of painting often seen in the past. This unframed oil-on-board painting is brighter (with more light), but the industrial cityscape is equally striking. And the haziness of the background may call to mind industrial pollution; the visible industrial chimneys trail smoke. The working-class nature of Christ is even more apparent in this painting, since his limp figure is shown wearing a flat cap, as are the three small figures in the street beyond. Although less animated in their movement than the people in the first painting, these three seem equally oblivious to the man hanging from the telegraph pole.

This is Christ's suffering for an industrial age. His identification with the powerless and downtrodden of industrial society, even if they do not recognize his revolutionary actions on their behalf, is striking.

The cross and the worker

Despite the turmoil of industrial development, there were those who sought to depict a noble view of labour, even as it was being subjected to dramatic change and ruthless exploitation. This sometimes took the form of nostalgia for earlier craft production, and sometimes encouraged contemporary workers to adopt what were considered positive social activities at a time when dehumanizing changes seemed to be prompting alarming tendencies towards vice in the dirty cities of the nineteenth century.

When William Holman Hunt painted *The Shadow of Death* between 1870 and 1873 *(Picture 12.4)* it proved to be very popular and consequently was widely reproduced as an engraving. Profits made from the sale of these prints allowed the donation of the original painting to Manchester City Art Gallery in 1883. In the painting we see Jesus resting from work in the carpenter's workshop. Standing upright and stretching tired arms, his shadow falls across a rack of tools fixed to the wall behind him. This combination produces the clear image of crucifixion: the shadow of death of the painting's title. The kneeling figure of Mary turns to look at the shadow on the wall; in doing so she looks up from a box in which she has kept the gifts given to the infant Jesus by the Magi (as recorded in Matthew's Gospel). A star shape in the frame above the window may also connect back to this earlier event.

Art critics have drawn attention to the messages encoded in this prediction of future crucifixion. The idea of Christ as a hard-working craftsman embodied the nobility of labour that was promoted by a number of Pre-Raphaelite artists (and also the Arts and Crafts Movement) in the face of de-skilling caused by mass production and machine-made industrial processes. This was also consistent with the contemporary views of Thomas Carlyle, who argued for the spiritual and moral benefits of manual labour.[6] The painting embodied the so-called Protestant work ethic.[7] The toned body of Christ – associated with his physical work – was also consistent with the writings of Charles Kingsley and Thomas Hughes, who promoted the virtues of physical health alongside the pursuit of Christian moral ideals in both personal and political life. In a similar parallel between contemporary views of what constituted ideal working-class behaviour and the painting, it is significant that Mary has saved the treasures given by the Magi. In this she exemplifies the honest toil and responsible thrift promoted as attributes that should be emulated by the working class.

Picture 12.4
The Shadow of Death, by William Holman Hunt, 1870–73, Manchester City Art Gallery.

Chapter 13

THE CROSS IN THE AGE OF TOTAL WAR

In an age of total war (an unrestricted war which impacts on all in society) civilians as well as soldiers suffer appallingly. The total dead of the First World War numbered somewhere in the region of twenty million (soldiers and civilians); the total dead of the Second World War about eighty million. These figures include both military casualties and deaths from war-related diseases and famine. The numbers are horrifyingly large and it is not surprising that these experiences have influenced ideas about the suffering of Christ as represented by the cross. This has affected both how Christ's suffering itself is represented and how human suffering is portrayed through reference to his suffering.

Picture 13.1

First World War Cross of Sacrifice, showing a sword superimposed on the cross, Tyne Cot Cemetery, near Ypres.

The cross and the impact of war on soldiers

Christ's cross came to be applied in two striking ways to the suffering experienced by soldiers fighting these terrible wars, especially in the First World War.

On one hand it became a model of sacrifice that could be used to make sense of the loss experienced by soldiers and their bereaved families. In this way, soldiers were seen as laying down their lives for country, families and friends, just as Christ had laid down his life for the world. The natural assumption that one's own side and cause is just only added potency to this approach. The clearest example of this is the so-called Cross of Sacrifice, which was placed in every cemetery into which forty or more bodies were gathered by the Imperial War Graves Commission (later the Commonwealth War Graves Commission, CWGC). It was designed in 1918 by Sir Reginald Blomfield *(Picture 13.1)*. A tall Latin cross, both its upright shaft and crossbar are octagonal in section. Attached to the front of the cross is a bronze longsword, with its blade pointing down. Some memorials also have a sword attached to the back. The sheer simplicity of this monument is striking and iconic, and was chosen over other competing (and more elaborate) designs. The cross is usually constructed from Portland stone (occasionally from granite) or other local white limestones. The largest Cross of Sacrifice in the world is the 12-metre-high one at the Halifax Memorial in Halifax, Nova Scotia, Canada.

On the other hand, the fact that Christ was innocent of crime, but suffered at the hands of an occupying power as the result of a conflict with the religious hierarchy of his day, could lead to the cross being deployed in a highly subversive way that challenged the whole idea of noble cause and sacrifice. The First World War poet Wilfred Owen wrote:

> *For 14 hours yesterday, I was at work – teaching Christ to lift his cross by numbers, and how to adjust his crown; and not to imagine he thirst until after the last halt; I attended his Supper to see that there were no complaints; and inspected his feet to see that they should be worthy of the nails. I see to it that he is dumb, and stands to attention before his accusers. With a piece of silver I buy him every day, and with maps I make him familiar with the topography of Golgotha.*[1]

For Owen, then, the cross was symbolic of a ruthless war machine that sacrificed men, just as Christ had suffered violence from the politically powerful. Not for him the noble sacrifice that was to be officially embodied in the Cross of Sacrifice.

The linking of the war dead to Christian sacrifice was not unique to the British. All the European nations involved in the First World War were Christian. In the Second World War the Nazi government officially paid lip service to Christianity, even though the Nazi Party was antagonistic to the Christian church. Most Germans considered themselves Christians in both world wars. The cemeteries now cared for by the German war graves agency, the *Volksbund Deutsche Kriegsgräberfürsorge* (VDK), are frequently marked with a cross. For example, several groups of three basalt-lava crosses stand among the flat headstones at Langemark Cemetery in Belgium.[2] A basalt-lava cross was also erected on one of the three surviving German bunkers that remain on this site. These bunkers were incorporated into the architecture of the cemetery.[3] In addition, the badge of the VDK consists of five combined crosses.

What is clear from the official use of the cross is that the symbol reflected the fact that these nations still considered themselves Christian. For this reason, on CWGC headstones a cross was inscribed on most war graves unless the commemorated soldier came from a different faith, such as Judaism or Islam, or if a family requested no symbol be engraved. The Star of David – containing the Hebrew for "May his soul be intertwined in the circle of the living", meaning union with the eternal God – appears on Jewish headstones. On Muslim headstones Qur'anic verses appear, such as, "We belong to God and to Him we shall return" (Qur'an 2.156).[4]

Most CWGC cemeteries have a Cross of Sacrifice, with the exceptions being where a majority of those buried are Chinese or Indian. As an echo of medieval antagonisms over the cross as a crusader symbol (see Chapters 7 and 19), none were placed on CWGC cemeteries in Turkey. Instead, a simple cross on a stone slab was placed at the back of the cemetery. This, of course, lacks what might be considered a "crusader sword". This brings us to a highly controversial issue…

Most CWGC cemeteries have a Cross of Sacrifice, with the exceptions being where a majority of those buried are Chinese or Indian. As an echo of medieval antagonisms over the cross as a crusader symbol, none were placed on CWGC cemeteries in Turkey.

The cross and the way the "enemy" was perceived

The cross in the CWGC context and on other British memorials also came to represent something of a crusade against injustice. The addition of the sword to the cross implicitly linked it to a concept of knightly conduct and even of "crusade" (in an era more comfortable with the use of that word). The architect Sir Herbert Baker (1862–1946), who contributed to the design for the Tyne Cot Cemetery in Belgium,[5] was pursuing the theme of crusade in his designs from 1917.[6] He even called the sword on his (rejected) submission for the Cross of Sacrifice a crusader's sword. He termed it the "Ypres Cross", named after the Ypres Salient in Belgium, where so many British and Empire troops fought and died.[7] He has been described as being "obsessed with the idea of a 'modern Crusade'".[8] In fact, in the minutes of a meeting of Imperial War Graves Commission architects, held in July 1917, the memorial cross was described "as a mark of the symbolism of the present crusade".[9] In a continuation of this theme the inscription on the reverse of the Allied Victory Medal reads "THE GREAT WAR FOR CIVILISATION, 1914–19".

The cross could also be deployed in order to explicitly associate the enemy with the Roman perpetrators of violence who crucified Christ. On an American Liberty Bond poster, published in the Philippines in 1917, the

Picture 13.2
First World War American Liberty Bond poster – showing an Allied soldier crucified by a German – by Fernando Amorsolo, published in the Philippines in 1917.

artist Fernando Amorsolo pictured an Allied soldier crucified by the Germans *(Picture 13.2)*. This linked back to the theme of noble sacrifice, while at the same time using it as a means by which the enemy could be depicted as evil. It also connected with a claim that a Canadian soldier's body had been discovered in 1915, crucified by Germans. Some accounts identified him as a sergeant; others claimed six men had died this way. Detailed investigation suggests that this claim is almost certainly without foundation, but it provided a powerful religious buttress to patriotism.[10]

The cross and the impact of war on civilians

The suffering of civilians, indeed of whole nations, could also be illustrated in such a way as to both parallel their pain with that of Christ and to present their persecutors as evil. The illustration of *Poland Crucified* by Sergey Solomko (produced c. 1915–17) is a dramatic example of this *(Picture 13.3)*. The fact that the personification of crucified Poland is a woman only serves to underscore the evil of the perpetrators of this act of violence. It should be noted that the painter has reduced the potential horror of the scene by showing her *bound* to the cross, and though her clothing is dishevelled and revealing, she is still largely clothed. She does, though, wear a crown of thorns.

During the First World War the crucifixion accusation included as victims: babies, children and US soldiers (after 1917), as well as the Canadian(s) already mentioned. The potency of extreme uses of the cross image has continued into the twenty-first century, particularly in communities that are familiar with Christian motifs. During the Russian–Ukrainian conflict in 2014, a story emerged of a refugee who had "witnessed" the crucifixion of a three-year-old child by pro-Ukrainian forces in Lenin Square, Sloviansk, in the violently contested Donetsk region of eastern Ukraine. The report, on Russia's main news channel *Novosti Perviy kanal*, in July 2014, made the parallel explicit when it described the child as being "nailed like Christ". Investigation revealed that the refugee was not from Sloviansk and, furthermore, there is no Lenin Square in that city.[11] Truth is often the first victim of war.

Perhaps *Picture 13.4* sums up the theme most completely. Photographed by a young German soldier, it simply identifies Christ with his suffering world in the age of total war.

Picture 13.3
Poland Crucified, postcard by Sergey Solomko, c. 1915–17.

Picture 13.4
Crucifix and war dead, photographed by the German soldier and photographer Walter Kleinfeldt, 1917.

Chapter 14

THE SUPREME SACRIFICE

From the Victoria Cross to the *Croix de Guerre*, from the Iron Cross to the Distinguished Service Cross, the sacrifice associated with the Christian cross is reflected in the military medals and orders of the nineteenth to the twenty-first century across the world.

Among nations with a Christian heritage the cross is a well-established symbol of religious identity and sacrifice. It features on flags and coats of arms and it is no surprise that it also features in the design of military medals awarded for bravery and self-sacrifice. While this ultimately connects with Christ's self-sacrifice, the iconic shape is so engrained into the history and outlook of these nations that the appropriateness of the symbol will unconsciously recommend itself to people, even if they do not actually make the ultimate mental connection with Christ.

Among nations with a Christian heritage the cross is a well-established symbol of religious identity and sacrifice. It features on flags and coats of arms and it is no surprise that it also features in the design of military medals awarded for bravery and self-sacrifice.

Germany

The famous Iron Cross medal (*Eisernes Kreuz*) was first instituted in the kingdom of Prussia by King Friedrich Wilhelm III in 1813, during the Napoleonic Wars. It later became famous during the years of the German Empire (1871–1918) and during the period of Nazi Germany (1933–45). The medal took as its distinctive form the *Schwarzes Kreuz* (black cross). This was the emblem of the Prussian Army and, after the formation of a unified state, the army of Germany from 1871. The angled arms of this *Schwarzes Kreuz* give it a distinctive appearance. During the period 1918 to 1945 it gave way to the so-called *Balkenkreuz* (literally "bar cross", a straight-armed cross) as a military symbol, but since 1956 the angled *Schwarzes Kreuz* has once again become the symbol of the German military, the *Bundeswehr*.

Inaugurated during the Prussian campaign against Napoleon, the Iron Cross medal *(Picture 14.1)* was the first military decoration that was open to all ranks, including enlisted men. From this time onwards the same black cross also appeared on the flag of Prussia. It was inspired by the form of cross used as a symbol by the crusading order of the Teutonic Knights in the Middle Ages. As such, it seemed a fitting symbol to represent military courage and self-sacrifice. The cross was originally issued in two classes, with the Iron Cross First Class being for the bravest acts. To achieve the First Class, a soldier had to have previously been awarded the Second Class award. A higher award – the Grand Cross – was only awarded to senior generals of the Prussian (and later German) Army. The Iron Cross was awarded again from 1939, but this time another grade had been added between the First Class and the Grand Cross: this was the Knight's Cross of the Iron Cross. The Knight's Cross was itself awarded in five grades: Knight's Cross, Cross with Oak Leaves, Cross with Oak Leaves and Swords, Cross with Oak Leaves, Swords and Diamonds, then finally one with Cross, Golden Oak Leaves, Swords and Diamonds. The Iron Cross was awarded in much higher numbers than the British Victoria Cross.

Picture 14.1

The German Iron Cross. Instituted in 1813.

Muslim members of the SS who were awarded the medal wore only the ribbon, due to Islamic objections to the cross as a symbol. The only person to be awarded both the Iron Cross and the Victoria Cross was William Manley, who served in an ambulance unit during the 1870–71 Franco-Prussian War and was also a British army officer and a surgeon. The youngest person awarded the Iron Cross (Second Class) was twelve-year-old Alfred Czech, during the Battle of Berlin, 1945.

The German *Bundeswehr*'s Cross of Honour for Valour, instituted in 2008, replaced the award of the Iron Cross, which was terminated as an award in 1945.

The United Kingdom

The highest award for military bravery is the Victoria Cross (VC) *(Picture 14.2)*. It was instituted in 1856. The metal for most of the medals awarded came from cannons captured from the Russians in 1855, during the Crimean War. Hancocks jewellers of London have been responsible for the production of every VC awarded. The youngest persons awarded the VC were aged just fifteen: Thomas Flinn, in 1857, during the Indian Mutiny, and Andrew Fitzgibbon, in 1860, at the capture of the Taku Forts, China.

Comparable, as a "Level 1 decoration", is the George Cross (GC). Instituted in 1940, it is for bravery other than in actual combat. In 1942 the entire island of Malta was collectively awarded the GC for bravery in the face of intense bombing by the Germans and Italians. Consequently, it still appears on the Maltese flag. The only other collective awarding of the GC was to the Royal Ulster Constabulary in 1999, in recognition of its role in counter-terrorism operations in Northern Ireland.

Below this tier the Distinguished Service Order (DSO) was instituted in 1885 for meritorious or distinguished service by officers in wartime. It is a white enamelled cross. Between 1914 and 1916 awards of the DSO included staff officers who were not in actual combat, and this caused resentment among front-line officers. Consequently, from 1917 the recipient had to have been "under fire" from the enemy. Since 1993, this medal has been awarded only for distinguished *service* (leadership and command) by *any army rank*. The Conspicuous Gallantry Cross (a silver cross) was at the same time introduced as the second highest award for *gallantry* after the VC.

Picture 14.2
The British Victoria Cross. Instituted in 1856.

The tier of medals below this includes: the Distinguished Service Cross, instituted in 1901 (originally as the Conspicuous Service Cross); the Military Cross, instituted in 1914; the Distinguished Flying Cross (DFC), instituted in 1918; and ranked below the DFC is the Air Force Cross, instituted in 1918. These four medals were awarded to officers only, until 1993.

Exceptional services in military nursing are rewarded by the Royal Red Cross, instituted in 1883 and awarded in two classes.

The sheer number of cross medals indicates how deeply engrained in British military iconography the cross has become as a symbol of courage, service and self-sacrifice.

France

The *Croix de Guerre* (cross of war) was established in 1915 and continues to be issued by France for acts of courage (*Picture 14.3*). It is a square-cross medal, with angled arms, on two crossed swords. The *Croix de Guerre des théâtres d'opérations extérieurs*, abbreviated to the *Croix de Guerre TOE*, is awarded for combat in foreign countries.

During the Second World War there were no fewer than four versions of the *Croix de Guerre* in existence due to awards made in the period 1939–41, before being abolished by the Vichy government, and then the existence of three rival seats of French government in London (which in 1944 revived the 1939 medal), in Vichy and in Algeria, all of which issued versions of the medal.

Another medal, the Cross for Military Valour, was instituted in 1956, and is awarded in conflict areas for which the *Croix de Guerre TOE* is not considered appropriate. As such, the Cross for Military Valour is usually awarded for security or peacekeeping operations that occur beyond French territory.

A reasonably similar *Croix de Guerre* medal was also instituted by Belgium in 1915. However, the Belgian medal is in the form of a Maltese cross, with balls at its eight points. It is surmounted by a royal crown.

Picture 14.3

The French *Croix de Guerre*. Instituted in 1915.

Picture 14.4
The American Navy Cross

The USA

In the USA the highest award for bravery is not in the shape of a cross. Instead, the Medal of Honor is star-shaped and so connects with the symbolism of the Stars and Stripes flag. However, the next tier down in terms of bravery awards is made up entirely of cross-shaped medals. These are: the Distinguished Service Cross (Army), the Navy Cross (Navy, Marine Corps, and Coast Guard) (*Picture 14.4)*, and the Air Force Cross. The Distinguished Service Cross was instituted in 1918 and was followed by the Navy Cross in 1919. Originally, the Navy Cross was lower in precedence than a medal termed the Navy Distinguished Service Medal. This was because the Navy Cross was originally awarded for both combat heroism *and* "other distinguished service". However, the US Congress revised this in 1942 by making the Navy Cross a combat-only award. This made it second only to the Medal of Honor as a naval award.

The USA also awards the Distinguished Flying Cross (DFC) for single acts of heroism, and also for extraordinary achievement during aerial combat. It was authorized in 1926. A famous civilian peacetime recipient was the transatlantic pioneer Charles Lindbergh.[1]

Other cross-shaped medals for military valour

Other modern military awards for bravery or other meritorious conduct, in the form of a cross, include:

Cross to the Heroic Valour in Combat (Argentina)

Military Merit Decoration (Austria)

Croix de Guerre, Military Decoration for Acts of Courage (Belgium)

Order of Military Merit (Brazil)

Valour Cross (Denmark)

Cross of Valour, Medal for Gallantry. The latter replaced the former in 1974, but has never been awarded (Greece)

Military William Order (Netherlands)

New Zealand Cross, instituted in 1999 primarily for civilians, but also for the military (New Zealand)

War Cross with Sword (Norway)

Order of *Virtuti Militari* (Poland)

Order of St George, established in 1769 and revived in 1992 (Russia)

Laureate Cross of St Ferdinand (Spain)

Gold Cross of Zimbabwe, which replaced the Grand Cross of Valour in 1980 (Zimbabwe)

Picture 14.5

The Belgian Deportation Cross, for those sent as forced labour to Germany in the First World War.

Chapter 15

THE ABUSE OF THE CROSS (FASCISM AND RACISM)

Between 1919 and 1945 Europe saw the rise of racist nationalist parties that between them either caused or collaborated with appalling crimes, including racial genocides unparalleled in history. What is shocking is how a number of these groups involved the cross in their symbolism.

Given the officially Christian nature of many European societies in this period, and the long history of Christian culture in Europe, this is not surprising. The cross had become deeply engrained into European symbolism and was closely associated with national identities, established churches, popular culture and traditional family values. It is therefore not surprising that it was appropriated by groups claiming to be defending these. This was especially so given fears concerning Soviet Communism, which was explicit in its antagonism to all of these things. In this way, opposition to Bolshevism was frequently presented as defence of "Christian values", even when it was articulated by groups whose beliefs and values were in stark contrast to Christian principles. Sadly, a church tradition of anti-Semitism in many countries only added to this process (despite the Jewish nature of Christ and the roots of Christianity). It was in protest at this tradition of Christian anti-Semitism that Chagall produced *White Crucifixion* in 1938, which reminded viewers of the Jewish nature of Jesus by picturing Christ as a recognizably Jewish martyr[1] *(Picture 15.1)*. His loincloth is a prayer shawl, his crown of thorns is replaced with a headcloth, the four figures mourning him wear traditional Jewish clothing. Around the scene of crucifixion are images of violent pogroms. The message is clear: the anti-Semites are identified as tormentors of Christ the Jew.[2]

Picture 15.1
White Crucifixion, by Marc Chagall, 1938. Art Institute of Chicago, Chicago.

Into this flowed another stream that was independent of Christianity, for cross-like symbols were also associated with a number of ancient cultures. Some of these symbols were prehistoric and pagan. Others – while having associations with other world religions such as Hinduism – had complex roots that had also influenced symbolism in Europe.

I.N.R.I.

In these ways the racist nationalist groups could, paradoxically, pose as defenders of "Christian civilization" while also claiming to embody identities that were pre-Christian. Depending on their target audience they stressed one or other at different times; or attempted fusions of the two.

A number of modern neo-Nazi and neo-fascist groups (from Russia to the USA) use these or variants of these symbols (or ones derived from them).

Germany: the Nazis

The swastika is now so associated with the Nazis it is easy to forget that it is an ancient religious symbol still used on the Indian subcontinent and elsewhere in Asia. It can also be seen stamped on Anglo-Saxon cremation pots and was used as a symbol in many ancient Germanic cultures and in the Late Roman military. Consequently, it can be found in areas as diverse as the prehistoric Indus Valley Civilization and in Mesopotamia, and also in Byzantine and Christian artwork. From the Middle Ages it has gone under a number of names in Europe: *cross cramponnée*, *croix gammée* (due to perceived similarity to four Greek uppercase *gamma* letters combined), *fylfot*, gammadion cross, *Hakenkreuz*, tetraskelion. A swastika is a symmetrical equilateral cross, but is distinct in having all four arms bent at 90 degrees. It usually appears clockwise (or right-facing) but can also be anti-clockwise (or left-facing) in shape when, technically, it is a *sauvastika*. The former is more common in Hinduism and the latter in Buddhism.

The name swastika is derived from a Sanskrit word associated with good fortune. The symbol is still used in Hinduism and also in Buddhism and Jainism. Across medieval Europe it appeared on coats-of-arms and in church architecture due to its connection with the Christian cross. This Christianized a pre-existing auspicious symbol. Early ones can be seen as far apart as St Sophia church in Kiev, Ukraine, and the Basilica of St Ambrose in Milan, Italy. Three can be seen embroidered on the stole of a priest in the 1445–50 painting entitled the *Seven Sacraments Altarpiece*, by Rogier van der Weyden. Its use continued in Renaissance and Baroque art and architecture.[3]

When it was discovered by nineteeth-century archaeologists being used at the site of ancient Troy it soon became associated with the perceived migrations of so-called Proto-Indo-Europeans, who were considered by linguists at the time to have spoken the forerunner of Indo-European languages (a family of languages stretching from western Europe to India). In Germany and elsewhere it rapidly became romantically linked to ancient German tribes, Homer's

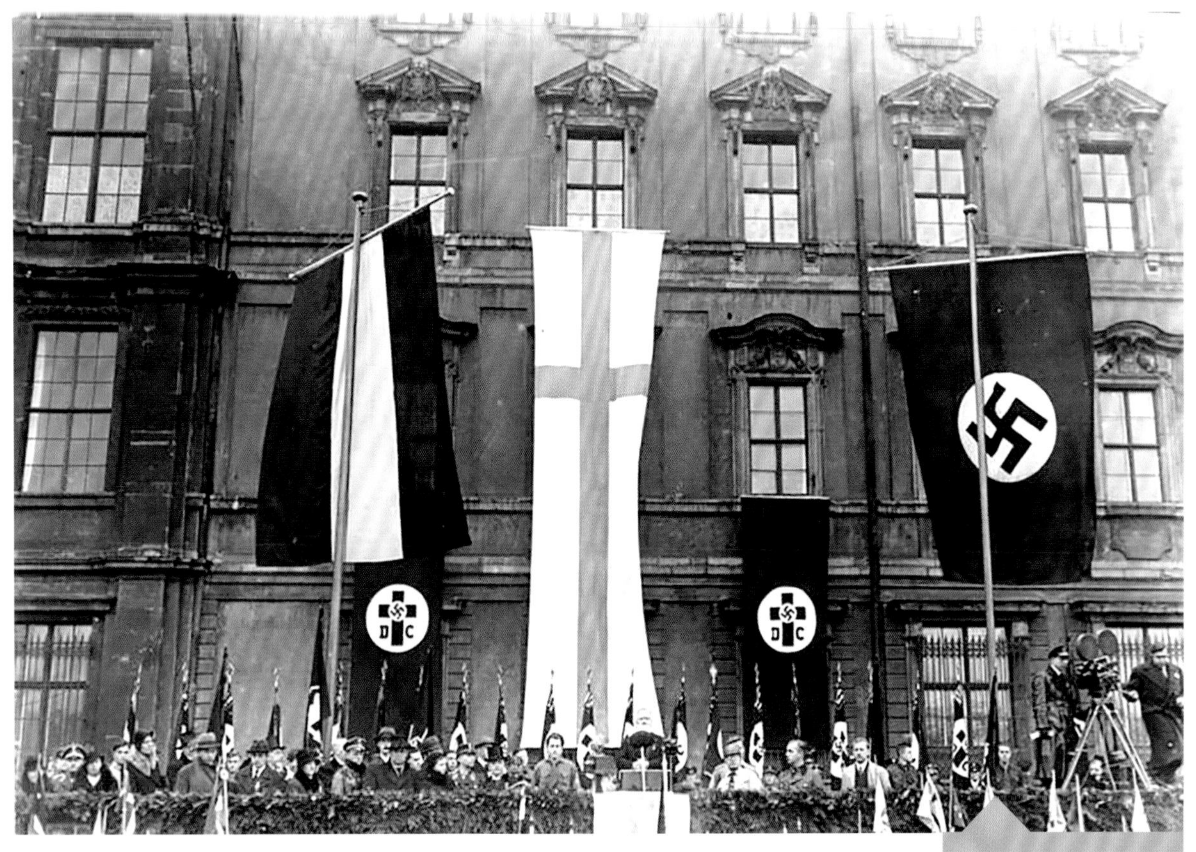

Picture 15.2
Christian cross and Nazi swastika combined at celebrations in honour of the 450th anniversary of the birth of Martin Luther, Berlin, 1933.

Greeks (c. 1200 to c. 800 BC) and Vedic India (c. 1500 to c. 500 BC). A more sinister use was by German *völkisch* (racial national) groups, who took it as a symbol of an imaginary "Aryan race", a Germanic/Nordic "Master Race".

In the aftermath of the First World War its familiar use among German nationalists was further encouraged by returning ex-soldiers who had used it painted as a symbol on their helmets while fighting Bolsheviks in the Baltic States. In 1920 Hitler took it as the symbol of the recently formed Nazi Party. This was a black (clockwise) swastika, which was rotated 45 degrees and placed on a white circle on a red background. In the 1930s there were attempts to have it replace or accompany the traditional Christian cross in (Nazified) German churches as part of an attempt to remove Jewish influences *(Picture 15.2)*. Hitler, like many Nazi leaders, mentioned God a lot but was really something of a neo-pagan, combining this with intense racist beliefs. Consequently, the swastika reassured traditional German Christians while appealing to the basically anti-Christian Nazi Party enthusiasts.

Picture 15.3
Hungarian Arrow Cross banner, 1944.

Hungary: the Arrow Cross

What later became the Arrow Cross Party was originally founded by Ferenc Szálasi in 1935 and called the Party of National Will.[4] Reformed in 1939 as the Arrow Cross Party, it was a national racist party modelled on the German Nazis. Its symbol was similarly ambiguous. It was formed from two green double-ended arrows combined as a cross and placed on a white circular background. This is known as a cross barbee *(Picture 15.3)*. An ancient symbol of the Magyar tribes of Hungary, it alluded to both racial and Christian identity.

As allies of the Nazis, the Arrow Cross briefly ruled Hungary from October 1944 to March 1945 and, in that capacity, murdered thousands of Jews and also Roma and Serbs.

Austria: the Fatherland Front

This party ruled Austria from 1933 to 1938 (when the Nazis absorbed Austria and removed it from power). Its symbol was the crutch cross or cross potent. It has crossbars or "crutches" at the four ends. In German, it is known as a *Krückenkreuz*, the "crutches cross". It had been used as a symbol of the Austrian First Republic in 1924. In 1934 it became the symbol of an Austria that became a fascist state under Chancellor Dollfuss and the authoritarian and traditionalist Catholic party the Fatherland Front. Its Catholic character was reinforced by the similarity of the crutch cross to the Jerusalem Cross and, as such, it was anti-Nazi (the government feared a Nazi seizure of power) *and* anti-Communist. The symbol it chose did not have the pagan connotations of the swastika.

Romania: the Iron Guard

In Romania the symbol chosen by the racist Iron Guard was a triple cross. This comprised three parallel vertical bars crossed by three parallel horizontal bars (standing for prison bars and martyrdom), usually in black. It was sometimes called the Archangel Michael Cross, whom the movement claimed as its patron saint. The Iron Guards were anti-Semitic extreme nationalists. They were fiercely anti-Communist and promoted the Orthodox Church.

When the anti-Semite Ion Antonescu came to power in Romania in 1940, he brought the Iron Guard into the government, which then carried out murderous attacks on Jews. In January 1941, a revolt of the Iron Guard was crushed and it was destroyed as an organization, but many of its members continued to support the Antonescu government and carried out horrific murderous pogroms of Jews until Romania finally left the war in 1944, in the face of Soviet advances.

Between 1919 and 1945 Europe saw the rise of racist nationalist parties that between them either caused or collaborated with appalling crimes, including racial genocides unparalleled in history. What is shocking is how a number of these groups involved the cross in their symbolism.

Bulgaria: the Ratniks

Founded in 1936 this paramilitary anti-Semitic group was similar to the Nazis, but it was also a supporter of the Bulgarian Orthodox Church. The Ratniks' badge was the *bogar*, or Bulgarian sun cross. This was an equilateral cross inside a circle. The name "sun cross" is derived from the assumption that it was a solar symbol, as it is found in many prehistoric pagan cultures.

King Boris III of Bulgaria dissolved the organization in 1939, but the ban was not enforced. And in September 1939 the Ratniks smashed Jewish shop windows in Sofia while the police looked on. As the Soviets advanced into Bulgaria in 1944, the Ratniks largely collapsed as a group. Some volunteered to fight for the Germans, while others fought the Communists.

Norway: National Unity

The Nasjonal Samling (NS) was a Norwegian fascist party active from 1933 until 1945. Founded by the former Norwegian minister of defence, Vidkun Quisling, its symbol was a golden sun cross on a red background. The sun cross was associated with Olaf II, patron saint of Norway. From 1940 the NS collaborated with the Nazi occupation of Norway.

The blazing crosses of the Southern USA

In the USA the racist cause was alarmingly mainstream in the form of the Ku Klux Klan. Founded after the Civil War, it was anti-black, anti-Catholic and anti-Semitic. It had a resurgence in the 1920s and again from the 1950s. Unlike the racist groups of Europe it was adept at operating within the political system of the USA, especially in the Southern states. Its use of violence and intimidation was associated with blazing crosses after 1915 *(Picture 15.4)*. This symbol of God's love had shockingly become a symbol of racism and intolerance when abused by the racist groups of the 1930s.

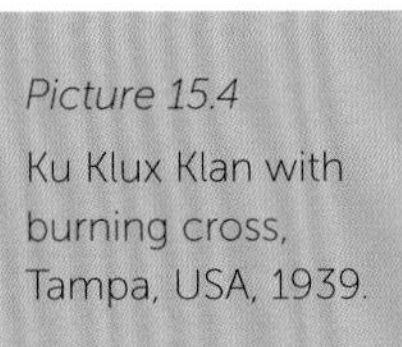

Picture 15.4
Ku Klux Klan with burning cross, Tampa, USA, 1939.

Chapter 16

THE MAN ON A VILLAGE TREE: THE PERSECUTED IDENTIFYING WITH THE CROSS IN THE POST-WAR WORLD

Given the nature of crucifixion, it is not surprising that it has become associated with groups experiencing persecution and marginalization. From the many possible examples, we will look at four groups for whom the cross has been presented as a symbol of their suffering and also their liberation: Dalits in India, Coptic Christians in Egypt, women generally, and African Americans.

Dalits identifying with the cross

"Our cries for liberation from harsh caste-bondage Were heard by God, who came to us in Jesus Christ… Jesus Christ is our Lord, Saviour and Liberator."

Within the Hindu caste system, Dalits are the so-called polluting "untouchables", existing in poverty outside the hierarchy of religious purity. In the 1970s, poor and outcast Christians adopted this name (in Sanskrit meaning "broken") as an expression of their oppressed status within Indian society, and also within the minority Indian Christian community over 400 years. The Indian church, which under the Roman Catholic missionary Roberto Nobili (1577–1656) had arguably originally identified itself with the ruling classes of India, accepted caste divisions as normative for society. Despite attempts by missionaries working among lower caste communities, Christianity appeared inaccessible to untouchables. However, between 1975 and 1986 a new Liberation Theology arose, centred upon Dalit problems with regard to poverty and discrimination.

The crucified Christ is central to Dalit theology, as they see in Jesus' crucifixion his full humanity. Christ is understood as a Dalit both in his suffering to redeem humanity and also in his apparent God-forsakenness upon the cross; the cross symbolizes the *dalitness* of divinity and humanity.[1] This "Dalit Christology" affirms the Dalit serving position as privileged. It is in suffering that Dalits know Christ, as they too live as "liberated servants" in whom God's salvation manifests itself.

Picture 16.1
The Man on a Village Tree, by Susheila Williams, Tamil Nadu, India.

These lines from the Christian Dalits' creed vividly present this outlook:

> *Our cries for liberation from harsh caste-bondage*
> *Were heard by God, who came to us in Jesus Christ…*
> *Jesus Christ is our Lord, Saviour and Liberator.*[2]

This identification with Christ is vividly portrayed in the painting entitled *The Man on a Village Tree (Picture 16.1)*, by Susheila Williams from Tamil Nadu, India. It depicts how Christ was not only alongside the poor and oppressed of his day as recorded in the gospels, but still suffers with the poor, low-caste villagers in the rural areas of contemporary India. The crucified Christ is presented as their personal saviour, liberator and humanizer, initiating a new social order by resisting the old discriminating hierarchies.

Coptic Christians identifying with the cross

In Egypt, Coptic Christians are in the minority (around 10 per cent), with most of the population being Muslim. The term "Copt" is often used of a Christian of any denomination who is of Egyptian descent living in Egypt or abroad. Most are members of the Coptic Orthodox Church of Alexandria; others are members of the Coptic Catholic Church. Smaller numbers live in Sudan and in Libya.

The Coptic Cross is made up of two equal-length lines that cross in the middle at right angles. At the end of each line are three points, representing the Trinity (the Father, Son and Holy Spirit). Overall, the cross has twelve points, representing the apostles who were to spread the Christian message worldwide.

Most Coptic Christians in Egypt have a small cross tattooed, usually on the inside of their right wrist, as a permanent, unashamed sign of their faith *(Picture 16.2)*.[3] These tattoos are not a fashion statement but a faith statement, and a reminder of how intimately Christian identity is bound to the cross as a symbol.[4]

As well as being a proud declaration of faith, such tattoos – which clearly mark out who is a Christian – are also important for security reasons. Due to escalating terrorist attacks on Christians and churches within Egypt, it is not uncommon for churches to have security at their doors checking people's wrists to see who is a Christian before they enter. Therefore someone must prove they are a Christian using their ID card (which displays their faith) before a Copt tattoo artist will apply the tattoo.

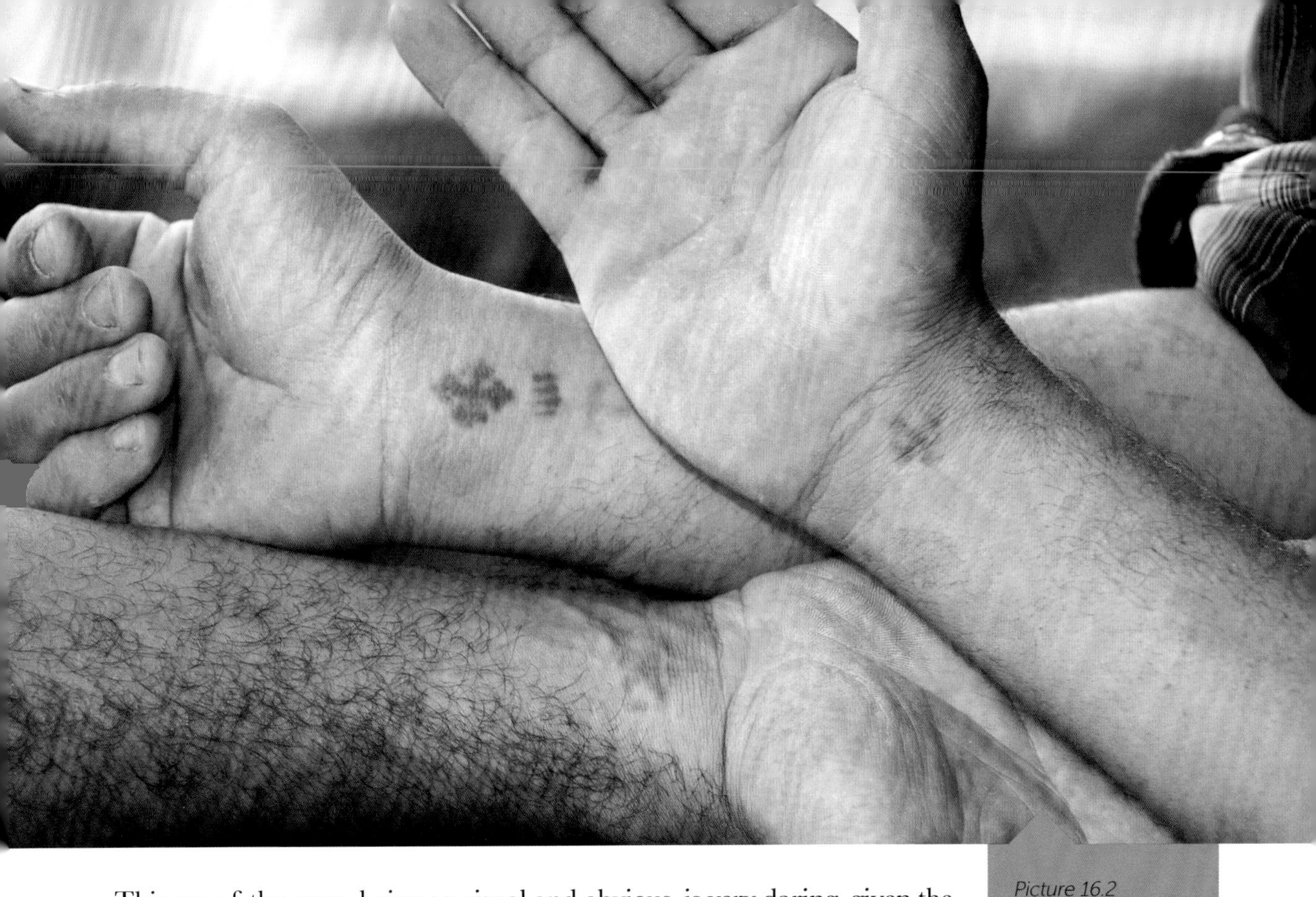

Picture 16.2

Cross tattooed on the wrists of members of the Egyptian Coptic Christian minority.

This use of the cross, being so visual and obvious, is very daring, given the discrimination and persecution that Copts have experienced at the hands of both Islamist extremist groups and, at times, the authorities. However, for Copts, having this cross etched into their skin is a way of sharing in the pain that the crucified Jesus felt; an identification with not just their religion but with their saviour. For Copts, the tattooed cross is a living sign of their faith, identity and commitment. It represents both the ostracism and the suffering they have undergone because of their relationship with the crucified Christ.

Women identifying with the cross

Gender roles in the church have historically been a topic of heated debate, particularly coming to the media forefront in 2014 when the Church of England voted allowing women to become bishops. The Catholic Church still insists on an all-male priesthood. Women challenging traditional conventions cite examples of inequality, such as: the church teaching that men are head of the family; some churches not allowing women to preach; and churches that use exclusively male language for God, despite God being ultimately beyond gender in Christian theology. They argue that the whole

Picture 16.3
Jesus Meets the Women of Jerusalem, by Bro. Mickey McGrath

of human experience and identity (male and female) needs to be seen in how we understand and view Christ. These debates rage on.

However, the matter goes further than debates about gender stereotyping and gender equality within the church. For in wider society across the globe, women often bear the brunt of male violence (at times in the most horrific forms) and economic and social discrimination. This has led to many such Christian women, reflecting on this suffering, to find particular solace in the suffering of Christ on the cross. Some would argue that while the crucified Christ was a man, this was culturally necessary to ensure Jesus could complete his mission, rather than representing any superiority of men over women. This presents the cross as a portrayal of (and identification with) female as well as male suffering, to equalize rather than elevate patriarchal power. A highly controversial example of this view can be found in the artwork *Christa*, a bronze sculpture of a female crucified Christ created by Edwina Sandys in 1975. It is the first of its kind in sculpture form. The face of Christ is shown as both suffering and compassionate. In 2015, Sandys explained that she did not make *Christa* as part of a specific women's rights campaign, but because she has always believed in gender equality. She stated that *Christa* is as relevant for Christians today as in 1975, and that the sculpture represents human suffering (female and male) and reveals "the journey of suffering that we all have in common".The sculpture continues to be highly controversial since its installation in the episcopal Cathedral of St John the Divine, New York, in 2015.[6] In contrast, other artistic expressions of Christ's relationship with women, as seen throughout his ministry *(Picture 16.3)*, celebrate his love for women and liberation of them.

Black Christians identifying with the cross

Another form of Liberation Theology is Black Liberation Theology or Black Theology, which originated among African American academics and some North American black churches. It later spread to other parts of the world, such as South Africa during apartheid. This theology views Christianity through a civil rights lens to empower those of African descent to overcome the discrimination they face because of their skin colour.

Black Theology sees the crucified Christ as the liberator of black people from oppression through his righteousness. In his life and death, God becomes incarnate and suffers alongside the persecuted. The crucifixion of Jesus on the cross runs parallel with the history of black people being lynched on trees. Like many African Americans in the past, Jesus too was excluded, abused and killed.

Black Theology also objects to images of a white Jesus, both for being historically inaccurate (because Jesus was Middle Eastern) and because white is associated with their oppressors. The Black Theology movement (along with others) has argued that the crucified Christ is not confined to a single skin colour, but – as he is personal and died for all – he can be envisaged as of any skin colour; therefore the oppressed can see the crucified Christ as having their skin colour, to emphasize that they are not alone in their suffering.

The (North) African origins of Simon of Cyrene, who carried Jesus' cross, has inspired some portrayals of him as an African *(Picture 16.4)*. Cyrene was in, what is now, Libya. The account of Simon is found in all the gospels, except that of John. Some advocates of Black Theology even point to the book of Daniel, where the messiah's hair is said to be "like pure wool", to argue that Jesus may have had dreadlocks and therefore may have been black. However, most advocates of Black Theology acknowledge that Jesus was not of African descent, even if they might depict him in this way. The depiction is based on identification with him, not historical accuracy.

Picture 16.4

The Monument to Service by Alan Collins at Oakwood University in Huntsville, Alabama, shows Jesus with Simon of Cyrene.

Chapter 17

THE CROSS AS A FASHION STATEMENT

Since the year 690, when the Sixth Ecumenical Council of the Church ruled that all representations of the cross must display the body of Christ in its entirety, crucifixes as well as plain crosses have been worn by Christians.[1] In the 1160s crosses appeared for the first time in Catholic jewellery, at the end of rosary beads. Therefore, despite the initial reluctance among early Christians to portray the cross and crucifix, there has since been a long history of Christians wearing both plain crosses and crucifixes as an outward sign of their faith, identifying them as Christian. However, in the last century there has been a secular commodification of this Christian icon by the commercial fashion industry. Recent years have seen controversy regarding whether the cross, as a fashion piece, should be reserved just for Christians, or whether it is acceptable to be borrowed and used by secular fashion labels.

The cross as a fashion statement

In the twenty-first century, religious-themed fashion products, including the cross on jewellery and items of clothing, can be found in high street and online shops. Examples of such cross-inspired fashion pieces include the cross dress *(Picture 17.1)* and, more dramatic still, the cross boots *(Picture 17.2)*. These products have been inspired by designers such as Dolce & Gabbana and Emilio Pucci's Peter Dundas, who have showcased numerous pieces portraying religious icons and crosses in their fashion shows. In the 2012 autumn/winter show in Milan, Versace's collection included Byzantine jewelled crosses on corsets, dresses and polo necks, the cross embroidered on coats, and the cross etched onto leather. In the same year Lanvin adorned a clutch bag with a cross, alongside ornate crosses worn on long chains.[2] Furthermore, celebrities including Madonna, Lady Gaga, Katy Perry, Alicia Keys and Rita Ora have also reinforced this trend, wearing large crosses, and also religious icons on clothing. Rita Ora's Dolce & Gabbana Large Cross

Picture 17.1
A dress by Couturissimo at the Paris fashion week, autumn/winter 2016–17.

Picture 17.2

The cross as fashion? The iconic Versace boots are covered in crosses.

Drop Earrings are a striking example. However, within the fashion industry the cross has become detached from its original religious meaning.

This adoption of the cross by the fashion industry contrasts with a feeling among some Christians that their right to wear the cross as a faith statement is under threat; indeed some high-profile cases have involved believers at odds with their employers over the right to wear the cross as a faith statement. Whatever one's viewpoint on this, it is in striking contrast to the prevalence of the symbol's use in secular contexts.

Not surprisingly, some have questioned whether it is appropriate for this religious symbol and method of execution to be embraced by the secular fashion industry. In 2013, in the foreword to a new Christian book called *Looking Through the Cross*, by Graham Tomlin, the Archbishop of Canterbury Justin Welby argued that the cross and this "badge of shame" (given that crucifixion was such a terrible and dishonourable death) for early Christians has been trivialized and emptied of its power and religious meaning by such secular use within the fashion industry. Recognized by the early Christians as being the humiliating mode of execution of their saviour, such understanding, it is argued, is now lost in the world of fashion. Welby claimed that "a cross that has no weight is not worth carrying". He further stated that now, because of time, fashion and familiarity, the cross is seen simply as a beauty symbol rather than as a symbol of salvation.[3]

Dave Burke, Pastor at Bethany City Church, Sunderland, agreed with the archbishop, saying that the fashion industry turns meaningful symbols into meaningless symbols. In challenging this use, he recounted how he takes the opportunity to ask those wearing such items why they are doing so and whether they know what it means.[4]

Additionally, writer and historian Ann Wroe, while accepting that the cross can be worn as a piece of jewellery, asserted that if the wearer does not know the original meaning or importance of the cross, and wears it simply for aesthetic reasons, then such use is not acceptable, due to its "huge cosmic significance". Wroe has further argued that since people would not wear other modes of execution as jewellery, those who do so need to understand the impact and magnitude of this symbol.[5] Clearly, the cross has lost nothing of its ability to challenge and generate heated debate.

This controversy regarding the use of religious imagery in fashion is not confined to the cross, however. When David Beckham wore a $1,000 Dolce & Gabbana set of prayer beads on the cover of *Vanity Fair*, leading Catholics expressed concern at this use of the rosary as a fashion item. Additionally,

Hindus were unhappy when Roberto Cavalli produced a collection of bikinis decorated with images of Hindu gods and goddesses. Nevertheless, this borrowing of religious icons by the fashion industry, though controversial, looks set to continue.

Where fashion meets iconic symbolism

It can be argued that through such fashions the cross has become universally recognized, regardless of faith. And this perhaps bears witness to the way in which the symbol has permeated the visual traditions of many countries. It could be argued that Italian designers such as Dolce & Gabbana and Versace have *woven together* the worlds of religion and fashion, having been inspired by their country's rich Catholic tradition. This has not been done without thought, or with disrespect, or with the deliberate intention to take away the meaning of the cross, but rather because the cross is still central to their concept of culture and identity. The focus has shifted from the cross simply as a symbol of salvation to the beauty of the shape and its iconography. Arguably, what has made the cross so desirable and attractive to the fashion industry is its visual power as a positive symbol understood by many, without designers having to laboriously explain the meaning of their designs.

Arguably, what has made the cross so desirable and attractive to the fashion industry is its visual power as a positive symbol understood by many, without designers having to laboriously explain the meaning of their designs.

Therefore, while the number identifying themselves as Christian has declined in the Western world, there is still a culture and history of Christianity in the West that is referenced by this secular use of religious symbols. Arguably, the cross belongs to all who share in this culture and history, even if for many it no longer seems to have the same meaning that the church attaches to it.

Clearly, such a mixture of a traditional religious symbol and modern secular use throws up challenging issues. James Sherwood, a fashion journalist, asserted that the use of the cross within the fashion industry corresponds with the era of "pick and mix" religion that we now live in. He argues that celebrities (such as Catherine Zeta Jones, Liza Minnelli and Renee Zellweger) wearing a crucifix is an example of borrowing from Christianity, perhaps even seeing the icon as a talisman or protective force. Theo Fennell's fashion cross *(Picture 17.3)*, worth £25,000, which was worn by Liz Hurley,

Picture 17.3
Theo Fennell with a fashion cross, valued at £25,000. Featured in The Telegraph in 2005.

Picture 17.4

David Beckham's back tattoo: a cross-shaped guardian angel.

may offer an insight into this personalized use. Sherwood suggested that Liz Hurley's references to the public as "civilians" may demonstrate an "us and them" (celebrity vs the public) outlook and may suggest that some celebrities wear the cross (even if unconsciously) as a protective force in a potentially hostile world.[6]

Furthermore, the cross may also have caught the eye of some celebrities because it adds an air of tradition, even piety, to any look. Therefore, there still appears to be some discernible spiritual dimension to the use of the cross in the fashion world, even if this dimension is not recognized by all Christians. Perhaps there is an echo of belief in the power of the cross in this unlikely context, even if it is unconscious. David Beckham's guardian-angel back tattoo *(Picture 17.4)*, created by Louis Malloy in an Art Deco design, may be a case in point. The original tattoo did not have the wings and instead portrayed a bald man, head bowed and arms outstretched. While Beckham specifically said that he did not want the tattoo to look like the crucifix,[7] the resemblance to an image of the crucified Jesus is striking and intriguing.

Overall, regardless of how Christians feel about it, the iconography of the cross has caught the imagination of fashion designers in the twentieth and twenty-first centuries. Even within a secular industry, something of the iconic visual power of the cross has been recognized and celebrated, albeit controversially.

Chapter 18

THE CROSS IN MODERN ART AND INSTALLATIONS

It is not possible to comprehensively review the many and varied ways in which the cross has been portrayed and reinterpreted in modern art and installations. As art conventions have become increasingly fluid from the late nineteenth century onwards, this has exploded the boundaries of what is categorized as "art". At the same time, the shock quality of many works of art has increased. Given the central role of the cross in Christian belief and in art history it is not surprising that artists have focused on its reinterpretation. This has meant that it has occupied a place in secular as well as sacred contexts. In one sense this is not new. Its use as a knightly motif or a political symbol also overflowed the boundaries of religious use. But, arguably, it is in the secular "space" of modern art and installations that it has experienced some of its most controversial handlings and interpretations.

A matter of perspective

Crucifixion, seen from the Cross (Picture 18.1), by the French painter James Tissot (painted 1886–94), is a dramatically different reinterpretation of the crucifixion. Rather than adopting the traditional perspective – with Christ central to the depiction – this one views the scene from the perspective of Christ himself. In one sense it shifts the focus from Christ to those present at the event. This might be interpreted as representing a time (the nineteenth century) when the central tenets of the Christian faith were increasingly challenged and the church was no longer central in many cultures where it had once dominated thought. But in some ways such an interpretation is too simplistic, for in this depiction all eyes are still on Jesus. He is the centre of attention, devotion, speculation and interest. In the painting, the love shown by Mary Magdalene, the casual indifference of the soldiers and the critical judgment of the priests is as one might have expected from earlier portrayals. The message seems to be that Christ still captures attention, but it is attention from an increasingly mixed audience with differing agendas.

Picture 18.1
Crucifixion, seen from the Cross by the French painter James Tissot, painted 1886–94. Brooklyn Museum, New York.

This is in many ways consistent with a century that saw many Christian beliefs questioned but that, arguably, takes us back to the very heart of the first-century event itself.

The matter of perspective and the relationship of the cross to the context of the world continued to challenge artists and elicit varied responses. Salvador Dalí's *Christ of Saint John of the Cross (Picture 18.2)* was painted in 1951 and was purchased by the City of Glasgow in 1952. This iconic painting is now well known from prints and reproductions, but its purchase at the time was controversial, as some critics thought such purchases should focus more on local artists, while others were critical of the painting itself, as we shall see. Controversy has followed it and it has been damaged twice, once by a visitor with a sharp stone.[1] In 2009, it was voted Scotland's favourite painting, with 29 per cent of the vote.

Given the central role of the cross in Christian belief and in art history it is not surprising that artists have focused on its reinterpretation. This has meant that it has occupied a place in secular as well as sacred contexts.

Strikingly the painting has no depiction of nails, blood or a crown of thorns. Dalí later said that he saw the scene – with its arresting angle – in a dream. This Christ is in stark contrast to the realistic depictions of the later Middle Ages or in Baroque churches of the Counter-Reformation. It is as if Christ's will alone fixes him to the cross. And yet the painting is firmly within Christian tradition, for the design was based on a drawing by the sixteenth-century Spanish Catholic friar known as John of the Cross, which is now in the Convent of the Incarnation in Avila, Spain.

In many ways it is a painting for the mid-twentieth century. Dalí described it as derived from "a cosmic dream", representing the "nucleus of the atom". He "considered it 'the very unity of the universe', the Christ".[2] With its combination of traditional visionary imagery and mathematically precise dimensions, Dalí also described the result as "Nuclear Mysticism". It has been criticized as overly traditional, even kitsch and banal. Despite this, it is probably the most famous twentieth-century depiction of the crucifixion.

The shock of the new

Art has always had the ability to shock, and for many artists this has been high on their agenda. The cross, over the two millennia of its representation, has often provoked responses designed to seize attention in a controversial

Picture 18.2
Christ of Saint John of the Cross, by Salvador Dalí, 1951. Kelvingrove Art Gallery and Museum, Glasgow.

manner. One has only to think of "Alexamenos worships [his] God" of around the year 200 (see Chapter 1). On the other hand, for much of the time its representation and use has been devotional, in sharp contrast to the motivation behind that earliest representation of the event drawn on the Palatine Hill. This devotional nature has set boundaries for the way the cross has been portrayed. This is hardly surprising, since the key objective of such a devotional object is to prompt worshipful reflection and not offence. However, given the offensive nature of this form of execution, "offence" has never been far away (potentially at least). Nevertheless, it is when the cross is removed from a devotional context that its representation can be most shocking.

Picture 18.3
The crucifixion of Jesus, a modern art sculpture at The Cathedral of the Good Shepherd in Singapore

The 1974 performance art of Chris Burden, titled *Trans-fixed*, was highly controversial when it took place, but then its process was designed to elicit a response from those viewing. Indeed, some of his performances were even designed to be interrupted by viewers. This particular one involved considerable personal discomfort for the artist himself. He was *actually nailed* to a VW Beetle. He himself described the event: "Nails are driven through my palms onto the roof of the car. The garage door was opened and the car was pushed halfway out into the speedway".[3] David Bowie's song "Joe the Lion", referred to this performance by Burden.

It is not surprising that many were disturbed and bewildered by Burden's piece. To some, it appeared a tasteless parody of the sacred mystery that lay at the heart of Christian faith. Yet to others there was something profoundly revealing about a human being nailed to an object of consumerism so strongly associated with the modern world: the motor car. They speculated on "the social and theological meaning of his body and, by analogy, the broken human body".[4] Was it depicting the "angst of being" that some would argue is at the heart of human experience in a fallen world? If so, despite its secular context, the piece might have something to say about both the broken nature of contemporary society and Christ's identification with that very society. In which case, its message could resonate with many depictions from a devotional context.

In a similar way, a controversial Benetton advertisement of 1992 – featuring the face of an AIDs patient – has been likened to Andrea Mantegna's *The Dead Christ* (c. 1500). The Benetton designer Oliviero Toscani even described the scene as *"La Pieta"* ("pity" in Italian).[5]

More consistent with late medieval graphic depictions of the cross – and in many ways as shocking, perhaps, as Burden's work – is David Mach's coat-hanger crucifixion, *Die Harder*, installed in Southwark Cathedral during Lent in 2012 *(Picture 18.4)*. Its depiction of the agonizing physicality of crucifixion, though, is directly intended to represent Christ himself, rather than by analogy. The graphic nature appears very twenty-first century, until one recalls something of the shocking brutality and explicit pain that appeared in late medieval art and also in the Baroque crucifixions of the Catholic Counter-Reformation. Although Mach is a self-confessed non-believer, the depiction can be compared

A feature shared by a number of these modern images of the cross, in a Christian context, is their statement about the brutality of crucifixion. In this a modern devotional realism draws both on depictions from the past and on modern and shockingly stark styles.

Picture 18.4
Coat-hanger crucifixion, *Die Harder*, by David Mach. Installed in Southwark Cathedral during Lent, in 2012.

to an earlier period of devotional art, designed to remind the viewer of the cost of salvation.

Similarly exhibited in English cathedrals (in Canterbury Cathedral in 1999, and in Winchester Cathedral in 1999–2000), the massive paintings of the crucifixion by Marcus Reichert are arresting modern reminders of the terrible agony of Christ and the reality of his suffering in his human body. In *Crucifixion IX*, the exhausted face of Christ stares out as he hangs between the darkness of the sky and the darkness of the earth *(Picture 18.5)*. Richard Harries, the Bishop of Oxford, described it as being among the most disturbing crucifixions painted in the twentieth century. The American critic Donald Kuspit wrote, "The image of an isolated human being in the process of being annihilated by the world and his own anxiety is one that speaks to every person in our anomic society. What makes Reichert's crucified Christ modern is his angry incomprehension at his suffering."[6]

Picture 18.5
Crucifixion IX, by Marcus Reichert, 1991. In the collection of Dr Henry Ralph Carse, Eothen, Huntington, Vermont, USA.

Brutally devotional?

A feature shared by a number of these modern images of the cross, in a Christian context, is their statement about the brutality of crucifixion. In this a modern devotional realism draws both on depictions from the past and on modern and shockingly stark styles. A good example of this combination is the *Passion Façade* of Basílica i Temple Expiatori de la Sagrada Família, Barcelona, Spain *(Picture 18.6)*. Its dramatic and soaring location on the prominent tower of a major church proclaims its devotional nature, but its bone-like columns and stark angles are designed to convey something of the brutality of the event. In this way historic devotion and modern artistic styles meet in an arresting manner.

Picture 18.6

Passion Façade of Basílica i Temple Expiatori de la Sagrada Família, Barcelona, begun in 1987.

Chapter 19

THE FUTURE OF THE CROSS

Contemporary experiences of the cross suggest some of the ways in which depictions of and ideas about the cross may develop further in the twenty-first century. For the cross will continue to be the defining symbol of Christianity.

A symbol that unites – but also divides

Such a symbol is more than a global brand or badge. And for all its controversy, it remains rooted in an event that occurred on a Middle Eastern hillside two millennia ago. It has transcended race, colour, gender and institutions. For Christians it remains the most profound and controversial insight into God's love.

The 2,000 years of the story of the cross have revealed how this powerful symbol has united Christians around a core belief. But it remains a highly controversial symbol: think of how it would be considered today if it were an electric chair, a noose or a lethal injection syringe. It is no wonder then that such a unifying symbol is, at the same time, a shocking one that also divides.

A portrayal of the cross that continues to cause debate is that by the Mexican artist José Clemente Orozco (1883–1949).[1] His mural cycle entitled "An Epic of American Civilization" was painted from 1932 to 1934 at Dartmouth College, Hanover, New Hampshire. It graphically charts the impact of European (and Christian) settlement on the Americas. That it was painted by a left-wing Mexican artist only underscores its potential to provoke controversy, given tensions in the twenty-first-century USA regarding Latino immigration and relationships with Mexico. Consequently, in a number of ways these murals "continue to resonate with the challenging circumstances of our own time".[2]

His Panel 21, "Modern Migration of the Spirit", shows a militant Christ armed with an axe, who has chopped down the cross so that it lies among the fallen ruins of other religions and civilizations; behind this are the dark shadows

Picture 19.1

Panel 21, "Modern Migration of the Spirit", in the "Epic of American Civilization Mural", 1932–34, by José Clemente Orozco, Baker Library, Dartmouth College, Hanover, New Hampshire.

of weapons and the flames of war *(Picture 19.1)*. But how should we read this picture? For some it represents the cross as symbolic of an aggressive ideology that (in its particular American manifestation) has crushed opposing peoples and ideologies, and even undermined itself and its publicly declared values (the fallen cross).[3] Or is it that the revolutionary Jesus lays low all the philosophies and beliefs of the world, even including systems of dehumanizing industrial and political power that seek to deploy the cross in contradiction to his radical power?[4] Or is it bleaker, asserting that through human sinfulness even the hope of salvation offered by the cross is no longer available, since it has been rejected by the axe-wielding Christ himself?[5]

Because the cross has been so closely associated with Western-orientated culture, its pictorial representation can, at times, associate it with the power and influence of *that* culture rather than its original first-century context of suffering and humiliation. This painting suggests that it can be as ambiguous as it is potent.

The cross and a modern "clash of civilizations"?

Nowhere does this division more shockingly reveal itself than in modern-day conflicts involving radical Islamists. We have seen how the cross became an object of violent confrontation during the crusades. And in the twenty-first century that same area of divisiveness has emerged again as extreme Islamists have taken to describing Western states as "crusaders" – terminology inadvertently encouraged with words used by President George W. Bush in September 2001.[6]

Among these extreme members of one part of the Muslim community this has revived vitriolic language regarding the cross and those associated with it. When members of so-called Islamic State (ISIS) captured the Iraqi city of Mosul in June 2014 they swiftly tore down all crosses from Christian places of worship *(Picture 19.2)*. They searched Christian homes for the symbol and destroyed all those that they found. This accompanied a campaign of killing Christians. When an affiliated group murdered twenty-one Coptic Christian Egyptian migrant workers on a Libyan beach in February 2015, they described those beheaded as "people of the cross". The video of their murder that was released was explicitly directed at "crusaders". It was as if the Battle of Hattin (1187) had occurred the day before. For many who heard of this atrocity, though, it seemed rather that those who died had more in common with the suffering saviour that they followed than with the

Picture 19.2
The broken cross of a Christian church in Qaraqosh near Mosul in 2016, after Iraqi forces recaptured the town from ISIS.

image of Western military power that the killers sought to evoke through their terminology. In this, the reference to the cross seemed to have returned to its original roots of humble sacrifice; clearly not what the perpetrators intended.

They would, no doubt, have claimed that their actions reflected a Muslim belief that Jesus (Isa in Islam) will return to break the cross and kill the pigs.[7] "Pigs" refers to an animal considered unclean by Muslims but eaten by Christians. This implies the abolition of non-Islamic religions and specifically Christianity. ISIS claimed to be anticipating this. Even when presented as an end-time event that should not be anticipated by human actions prior to this, this Hadith tradition still illustrates the profound disagreement between Christianity and some in Islam over this symbol and its association with Jesus.

It is clear that some approaches to the cross in the twenty-first century are both violent and divisive. A symbol that prompted an anonymous opponent of Alexamenos to ridicule his adherence to a crucified God (c. 200) remains offensive to some who reject Christian beliefs concerning the cross of Christ. And yet this potent symbol also inspires actions designed to reconcile those divided by violence.

The cross as an enduring symbol of reconciliation

Today in Coventry Cathedral in the UK, the Charred Cross still stands in the ruins caused by Second World War bombing. Behind it the words "Father Forgive" are etched in gold letters on the stones of the wall *(Picture 19.3)*. The altar below it is constructed out of rubble from the bombed building. This cross, made in 1964, replaced the original, following its destruction in 1940, and is made from two charred beams lashed together.

It has become a symbol of peace and reconciliation on an international scale. The new cathedral also houses the Cross of Nails, formed from three nails from the roof truss of the old cathedral. Over 300 of these crosses now exist across the globe, each formed from three nails from the Second World War ruin, until these ran out and then further nails were produced in Germany as a further symbol of reconciliation. One can be found in the ruin of the Kaiser Wilhelm Memorial Church in Berlin, itself destroyed by Allied bombing. A replica can be seen in Berlin's Chapel of Reconciliation, part of the Berlin Wall Memorial, created in 1998.

Twenty-first-century school children, visiting Coventry Cathedral on Religious Study trips, are reminded of how for Christians these survivals from twentieth-century violence are now symbols of reconciliation between nations, because the cross was originally the means of reconciliation between people and God.

The cross as owned by all who suffer and yet hope

A neighbourhood in Tuscaloosa, Alabama, was reduced to rubble after a tornado swept through the community in April 2011. This occurred during the largest tornado outbreak ever recorded in the USA. At one point, this huge tornado was a mile and a half wide: it killed and injured a large number of people and destroyed homes. And yet, in its aftermath, somebody raised up a cross made from splintered timber over a wrecked home. From it hung

Picture 19.3
The Charred Cross at Coventry Cathedral, "blitzed" in the Second World War: "Father Forgive".

cloth reminiscent of the "Robed Cross" or "Shrouded Cross", used in some Christian depictions of the cross as a reminder of the scarlet cloak placed on Jesus by the Roman soldiers who scourged and mocked him before the crucifixion *(Picture 19.4)*.

It is a powerful reminder of how the cross continues to speak to many people: as a dramatic symbol of God's love in the face of the worst that can happen in life. Such a symbol of love, life and hope continues to resonate in the twenty-first century as powerfully as it has done in the previous 2,000 years. Such a symbol is more than a global brand or badge. And for all its controversy, it remains rooted in an event that occurred on a Middle Eastern hillside two millennia ago. It has transcended race, colour, gender and institutions. For Christians it remains the most profound and controversial insight into God's love.

Picture 19.4

Makeshift cross amid tornado destruction, Tuscaloosa, Alabama, 2011.

ACKNOWLEDGMENTS

We are very grateful to many people who have assisted in the writing of this book and in sourcing the visual images. We would especially like to thank our agent, Robert Dudley, and all at Lion Hudson, especially Jessica Gladwell, Joy Tibbs and Eva Rojas, for their help and support. We are also indebted to the theologians and historians whose work on the cross we have consulted. Esther's studies in the Theology department at Cambridge University provided a great many insights that assisted in the exploration of the evidence and its interpretation; her second-year studies on the evolution of the crucifix were particularly informative. We are grateful to Dr Tim Winter, of Cambridge University, for assistance regarding the Hadith. Mitha Bleasdale was particularly helpful in enabling us to track down the remarkable image *The Man on a Village Tree*, painted by her grandmother Susheila Williams. To them both, and for permission to include this painting, we are very grateful.

All errors, of course, are our own.

Martyn Whittock and Esther Whittock

REFERENCES

INTRODUCTION

1 1 Corinthians 1:23–24. The Holy Bible, New Revised Standard Version, Anglicized Edition, Oxford: Oxford University Press, 1995. All quotations from the Bible are from this version, unless otherwise stated.

CHAPTER 1: THE CROSS OF SHAME

1 Friedman, M., "In a stone box, the only trace of crucifixion", *The Times of Israel*, 26 March 2012. www.timesofisrael.com/in-a-stone-box-a-rare-trace-of-crucifixion/ (accessed August 2016)
2 Tzaferis, V., "Crucifixion – The Archaeological Evidence", www.biblicalarchaeology.org/daily/ biblical-topics/crucifixion/a-tomb-in-jerusalem-reveals-the-history-of-crucifixion-and-roman-crucifixion-methods/ (accessed August 2016). See also V. Tzaferis, "Jewish Tombs at and near Giv'at ha-Mivtar, Jerusalem", *Israel Exploration Journal* 20/1, 2 1970, pp. 18–32; N. Haas, "Anthropological Observations on the Skeletal Remains from Giv'at ha-Mivtar", *Israel Exploration Journal* 20/1, 2 (1970), pp. 38–59; and J. Naveh, "The Ossuary Inscriptions from Giv'at ha-Mivtar", *Israel Exploration Journal* 20/1, 2, 1970, pp. 33–37. For a different hypothesis as to the position of Yehohanan on the cross, see Y. Yadin, "Epigraphy and Crucifixion", *Israel Exploration Journal* 23, 1973, pp. 18–22.
3 Zias, J. & E. Sekeles, "The Crucified Man from Giv'at ha-Mivtar: A Reappraisal", *Israel Exploration Journal* 35, 1985, pp. 22–27.
4 Evans, C., "The Family Buried Together Stays Together: On the burial of the executed in family tombs", in C. Evans (ed.), *The World of Jesus and the Early Church: Identity and interpretation in early communities of faith*, Peabody, MA: Hendrickson, 2011, p. 92.
5 Tombs, D., "Prisoner Abuse: From Abu Ghraib to *The Passion of the Christ*", in L. Hogan & D. Lehrke (eds), *Religion and the Politics of Peace and Conflict*, Eugene, OR: Wipf and Stock, 2009, p. 191, note 61 on John 20:25.
6 Acts 12:7.
7 The original is in (crude) Greek letters: *Αλεξαμενος σεβετε θεον*.
8 Holden, J. M. & N. Geisler, *The Popular Handbook of Archaeology and the Bible*, Eugene, OR: Harvest House, 2013, p. 309; see also R. Bauckham, *Jesus and the God of Israel: God crucified and other essays on the New Testament's Christology of divine identity*, Milton Keynes: Paternoster, 2008.

9 Tschen-Emmons, J. B., *Artifacts from Ancient Rome*, Santa Barbara, CA: ABC-CLIO, 2014, p. 16.

CHAPTER 2: PEOPLE OF THE CROSS

1 1 Corinthians 1:23–24.
2 Galatians 3:13–14: "Christ redeemed us from the curse of the law by becoming a curse for us – for it is written, 'Cursed is everyone who hangs on a tree' – in order that in Christ Jesus the blessing of Abraham might come to the Gentiles, so that we might receive the promise of the Spirit through faith."
3 Ephesians 2:15–17.
4 Acts 2:23–24.
5 Matthew 10:38.
6 John 19:19.
7 An interesting commentary, and examination of some of the claims about it, can be found at: www.bede.org.uk/orpheus.htm (accessed January 2017)
8 The British Museum, Collection online: www.britishmuseum.org/research/collection_online/ collection_object_details.aspx?objectId=59616&partId=1 (accessed January 2017)

CHAPTER 3: "BY THIS CONQUER!"

1 Eusebius of Caesarea, *Vita Constantini* (Life of Constantine), I. 22.
2 Lactantius, *De Mortibus Persecutorum* (On the Deaths of the Persecutors), 44.
3 Greek: **ΧΡΙΣΤΟΣ**, Christos.
4 And this is the most literal reading of the description in Lactantius's account.
5 Hurtado, L., "The Staurogram in Early Christian Manuscripts: the earliest visual reference to the crucified Jesus?", in T. Kraus, *New Testament Manuscripts*, Leiden: Brill, 2006, pp. 207–26.
6 For an overview of the evidence relating to these "visions", see D. S. Potter, *The Roman Empire at Bay, AD 180–395*, London: Routledge, 2004, note 119, p. 667. For both accounts in translation, see C. White, *The Emergence of Christianity: Classical Traditions in Contemporary Perspective*, Minneapolis, MN: Fortress Press, 2011, pp. 97–98.
7 See E. Thunø, *Image and Relic: Mediating the Sacred in Early Medieval Rome*, Rome: L'erma Di Bretschneider, 2002, p. 14.

CHAPTER 4. REIGNING FROM THE CROSS

1 Gavrilyuk, P. L., "God's Impassible Suffering in the Flesh", quoting the translation by Walter Kirkham Blount (d. 1717), in J. F. Keating & T. J. White (eds), *Divine Impassibility and the Mystery of Human Suffering*, Grand Rapids, MI & Cambridge: Wm. B. Eerdmans, 2009, p. 130.
2 An interesting brief examination of this can be found in J. Y. Paoletti & G. M. Radke, *Art in Renaissance Italy*, London: Laurence King Publishing, 2005, p. 50.
3 The origins of the *crux gemmata* are explored in C. J. Hahn, *Strange Beauty: Issues in the Making and Meaning of Reliquaries, 400–circa 1204*, University Park, PA: Penn State University Press, 2012, pp. 79–81.
4 See E. Garrison, *Ottonian Imperial Art and Portraiture: The Artistic Patronage of Otto III and Henry II*, Farnham: Ashgate Publishing, 2012, p. 75.
5 Quoted in R. Viladesau, *The Beauty of the Cross: The Passion of Christ in Theology and the Arts, from the Catacombs to the Eve of the Renaissance*, Oxford: Oxford University Press, 2008, p. 11.
6 Recent research has indeed confirmed that the figure always had eyes shut.
7 Saxon, E., "Romanesque art and the Eucharist", in I. Levy, G. Macy & K. Van Ausdall (eds), *A Companion to the Eucharist in the Middle Ages*, Leiden: Brill, 2011, p. 274.
8 An examination of the genre of The Smiling Christ can be found in R. Viladesau, *The Beauty of the Cross*, pp. 65–69.
9 Intriguingly, an Islamic Sufi tradition stated that whereas John the Baptist was always weeping, Jesus was always smiling (see N. Robinson, *Christ in Islam and Christianity*, Albany: State University of New York Press, 1991, p. 54). Whether there was any connection between this tradition and the corresponding Christian tradition evidenced from Spain is difficult to say.

CHAPTER 5: THE CROSS AND THE INHERITORS OF ROME

1 Bruce-Mitford, R., *The Sutton Hoo Ship Burial: A Handbook*, London: British Museum Publications, 1979, pp. 99, 101.
2 See J. J. North, *English Hammered Coinage, Volume 1: Early Anglo-Saxon to Henry III, c. 600–1272*, London: Spink & Son Ltd, 1994.
3 www.bl.uk/onlinegallery/features/lindisfarne/carpetpages.html# (accessed January 2017)
4 Alexander, M. (trans.), *The Earliest English Poems*, London: Penguin Classics, 1977, p. 107.

5 We are grateful to the cathedral staff in Brussels for allowing us a private viewing of the reliquary, even though the treasury was shut. It was a moving and memorable experience.
6 One of thirteen surviving full-page miniatures in this manuscript.
7 Wilson, D. M., *Anglo-Saxon Art*, London: Thames and Hudson, 1984, pp. 172, 174.
8 Webster, L., *Anglo-Saxon Art*, London: British Museum Press, 2012, p. 188.
9 "Carolingian Art (c. 750–900)", www.visual-arts-cork.com/history-of-art/carolingian-art.htm (accessed January 2017)

CHAPTER 6: THE CROSS AND HAMMER (VIKINGS)

1 Other examples of the cross alone (without a figure) have been found on other sites; some fifty miniature silver crosses and 400 iron ones have so far been discovered from the Scandinavian Viking Age. See A. Winroth, *The Conversion of Scandinavia*, New Haven, CT & London: Yale University Press, 2012, p. 134.
2 http://en.vikingemuseetladby.dk/about-the-museum/news/extraordinary-find-denmarks-oldest-crucifix (accessed February 2017)
3 Ibid.
4 Chatterton Newman, R., *Brian Boru: King of Ireland*, Cork: Mercier Press, 2011, p. 93.
5 Winroth, A., *The Conversion of Scandinavia*, p. 134.
6 Anthony, D., *Entangled Christianities*, Cambridge: Cambridge Scholars Publishing, 2016, p. 65.
7 In the shape of a "T".
8 Winroth, A., *The Conversion of Scandinavia*, p. 134.
9 For an exploration of this portrait, see C. E. Karkov, *The Ruler Portraits of Anglo-Saxon England*, Woodbridge: Boydell Press, 2004, pp. 121–40.

CHAPTER 7: THE CHALLENGE OF ISLAM: CRUSADER CROSS, CRUSADER CHRIST?

1 In this context meaning Jews.
2 *The Qur'an* 4:157–58, M. A. S. Abdel Haleem (trans.), Oxford: Oxford University Press, 2010.
3 The term "People of the Cross" was used by Islamist terrorists to describe twenty-one Egyptian Christians beheaded in Libya in February 2015. Members of the so-called Islamic State (ISIS) destroyed all crosses on the domes of churches in the city of Mosul when they captured it in June 2014, and raided Christian homes in order to destroy crosses.

www.catholicnewsagency.com/blog/the-people-of-the-cross-are-taking-back-iraq/ (accessed May 2017)

CHAPTER 8: SUFFERING ON THE CROSS

1 Quoted in G. Every, *Christian Mythology*, Feltham: Hamlyn, 1970, p. 73.
2 Henderson, J., *Piety and Charity in Late Medieval Florence*, Chicago: University of Chicago Press, 1997, p. 114.
3 Quoted in R. Viladesau, *The Beauty of the Cross: The Passion of Christ in Theology and the Arts from the Catacombs to the Eve of the Renaissance*, Oxford: Oxford University Press, 2006, p. 157.
4 The Holy Bible, English Standard Version, London: Collins (anglicized edn), 2002. Originally published Wheaton, IL: Crossway Bibles, a division of Good News Publishers, 2001.
5 Viladesau, R., *The Beauty of the Cross*, reflecting on observations made by the American theologian Gerard S. Sloyan, p. 172. See also H. Van Os, *Art of Devotion in the Late Middle Ages in Europe 1300–1500*, London: Merrell Holberton, in association with Rijksmuseum, Amsterdam, 1994.

CHAPTER 9: THE CROSS IN AFRICA

1 Phillipson, D. W., *Foundations of an African Civilisation: Aksum and the Northern Horn*, 1000 BC–AD 1300, Addis Ababa: Addis Ababa University Press/ James Currey, 2014, pp. 94–95; Y. K. Mekonnen (ed.), *Ethiopia: The Land, Its People, History and Culture*, Dar es Salaam: New Africa Press, 2013, p. 28.
2 Bellagamba, A., S. E. Greene & M. A. Klein (eds), *African Voices on Slavery and the Slave Trade: Volume 2, Essays on Sources and Methods*, Cambridge: Cambridge University Press, 2016, pp. 52–53.
3 Werness, H. B., *Continuum Encyclopedia of Native Art: Worldview, Symbolism, and Culture in Africa, Oceania, and North America*, New York, London: Continuum, 2003, p. 80.
4 Sanneh, L. & M. McClymond (eds), *The Wiley-Blackwell Companion to World Christianity*, Hoboken, NJ: Wiley-Blackwell, 2016, p. 380.

CHAPTER 10: CRUCIFIX OR EMPTY CROSS? THE REFORMATION AND COUNTER-REFORMATION

1 See R. Viladesau, "The Cross in Early Renaissance Theology and Art", in *The Triumph of the Cross: The Passion of Christ in Theology and the Arts from the Renaissance to the Counter-Reformation*, Oxford: Oxford University Press, 2008.
2 For an example of the claims made about the relic of the cross and

the crucifix attached to the reliquary at the Shrine of the Holy Cross at Tallard, France (as reported by the later Protestant leader Guillaume Farel), see C. M. N. Eire, *War Against the Idols: The Reformation of Worship from Erasmus to Calvin*, Cambridge: Cambridge University Press, 1989, p. 9.
3 Scribner, R. W., *Popular Culture and Popular Movements in Reformation Germany*, London: Bloomsbury, 1988, p. 111.
4 Ibid., p. 112.
5 Heal, B., "The Catholic Eye and the Protestant Ear", in P. Opitz (ed.), *The Myth of the Reformation*, Göttingen: Vandenhoeck & Ruprecht, 2013, p. 325.
6 Ibid.
7 See A. Bamji, G. H. Janssen & M. Laven (eds), *The Ashgate Research Companion to the Counter-Reformation*, Abingdon: Routledge, 2016.

CHAPTER 11: NEW WORLD – NEW CROSS?

1 For an overview of traditions connected with the one at Chimayo, New Mexico, USA, see N. Brockman, *Encyclopedia of Sacred Places, Volume 1*, Santa Barbara, CA: ABC-CLIO, 2011, pp. 100–01
2 Muir, E., *Ritual in Early Modern Europe*, Cambridge: Cambridge University Press, 2005, p. 193.
3 For an examination of the contemporary practice of placing memorial roadside crosses generally, see H. J. Everett, *Roadside Crosses in Contemporary Memorial Culture*, Denton, TX: University of North Texas Press, 2002.
4 Sayer, C., *Arts and Crafts of Mexico*, San Francisco, CA: Chronicle Books, 1989, p. 52.
5 For an accessible overview of the use of the cross symbol in Native American culture, see www.warpaths2peacepipes.com/native-american-symbols/cross-symbol.htm (accessed August 2017)
6 Ibid.

CHAPTER 12: THE CROSS IN THE AGE OF IMPERIALISM AND INDUSTRIALIZATION

1 A summing up of common twentieth-century anthropological conclusions in A. Iriye & P. Saunier (eds), *The Palgrave Dictionary of Transnational History: From the mid-19th century to the present day*, Basingstoke: Palgrave Macmillan, 2016, p. 717.
2 Ibid.
3 Hastings, A., A. Mason & H. Pyper (eds), *The Oxford Companion to Christian Thought*, Oxford: Oxford University Press, 2000, p. 111.

4 O'Brien, P. K., *Atlas of World History*, Oxford: Oxford University Press, 2002, p. 205.
5 Ibid.
6 Bronkhurt, J., *William Holman Hunt: A Catalogue Raisonné*, New Haven, CT & London: Yale University Press, 2006, p. 226.
7 Arnold, D., *Cultural Identities and the Aesthetics of Britishness*, Manchester: Manchester University Press, 2004, p. 125.

CHAPTER 13: THE CROSS IN THE AGE OF TOTAL WAR

1 Quoted in J. Stallworthy, *Wilfred Owen*, London: Random House, 2013, p. 265.
2 It is one of just four First World War German cemeteries in the Flanders region. It contains 44,294 war dead.
3 www.greatwar.co.uk/ypres-salient/cemetery-langemark.htm (accessed June 2017)
4 *The Qur'an*, M. A. S. Abdel Haleem (trans.), Oxford: Oxford University Press, 2010. On headstones these verses will be in Arabic.
5 This is the largest British war cemetery in the world. It is on the site of the 1917 Battle of Passchendaele, near Ypres, Belgium. It was unveiled in July 1927 and contains 11,965 war dead.
6 Skelton, T. & G. Gliddon, *Lutyens and the Great War*, London: Frances Lincoln, 2008, p. 26.
7 Goebel, S., *The Great War and Medieval Memory: War and Remembrance in Britain and Germany, 1914–1940*, Cambridge: Cambridge University Press, 2007, p. 88.
8 Ibid.
9 Ibid., p. 88 and note 32.
10 Cook, T., "Black-heated Traitors, Crucified Martyrs, and the Leaning Virgin: The Role of Rumor and the Great War Canadian Soldier", in J. Keene & M. Neiberg (eds), *Finding Common Ground: New Directions in First World War Studies*, Leiden & Boston, MS: Brill, 2011, p. 32.
11 Gaufman, E., "Memory, Media, and Securitization: Russian Media Framing of the Ukrainian Crisis", in *Journal of Soviet and Post-Soviet Politics and Society: Russian Media and the War in Ukraine*, vol.1, no.1, 2015, p.153.

CHAPTER 14: THE SUPREME SACRIFICE

1 An accessible overview, plus photographs of medals, can be found at: www.mowwvandenberg.org/MedalsPage.htm (accessed June 2017)

CHAPTER 15: THE ABUSE OF THE CROSS (FASCISM AND RACISM)

1 See I. F. Walther & R. Metzger, *Chagall*, Köln: Taschen, 2000, p. 62.
2 www.artic.edu/aic/collections/artwork/59426 (accessed April 2017)
3 For a succinct overview of the use of this infamous symbol, see M. Quinn, *The Swastika: Constructing the Symbol*, London: Routledge, 2005.
4 For a short overview of its aims and history, see C. Blamires & P. Jackson, *World Fascism: A Historical Encyclopedia, Volume 1*, Santa Barbara, CA: ABC-CLIO, 2006, p. 58. For a more detailed examination, see P. Morgan, *Fascism in Europe, 1919–1945*, London: Routledge, 2003.

CHAPTER 16: THE MAN ON A VILLAGE TREE: THE PERSECUTED IDENTIFYING WITH THE CROSS IN THE POST-WAR WORLD

1 See A. P. Nirmal, "Towards a Christian Dalit Theology", in A. P. Nirmal (ed.), *A Reader in Dalit Theology*, Madras: Gurukul, 1991, p. 65.
2 Quoted in M. E. Prabhakar, "Christology in Dalit Perspective", in V. Devasahayam (ed.), *Frontiers of Dalit Theology*, Delhi: I.S.P.C.K., 1997, pp. 419–20.
3 Meinardus, O. F. A., *Two Thousand Years of Coptic Christianity*, Cairo: American University in Cairo Press, 2002, p. 266.
4 For an overview of the Copts, including their current position, see L. M. Farag (ed.), *The Coptic Christian Heritage: History, Faith and Culture*, London: Routledge, 2013.
5 Nettie Reynolds in conversation with Edwina Sandys, in 2015. See: https://feminismandreligion.com/2015/10/06/christa-interview-with-edwina-sandys-by-nettie-reynolds/ (accessed July 2017)
6 See "The Christa Project", www.stjohndivine.org/programs/christa (accessed July 2017)
7 Noviss, S., *Infinite Wisdom: A History of Christian Art*, Leicester: Troubador Publishing Ltd, 2012, p. 126.

CHAPTER 17: THE CROSS AS A FASHION STATEMENT

1 It should be noted that both plain crosses and crucifixes continued to be worn and used after this date.
2 www.standard.co.uk/fashion/sign-of-the-cross-7585169.html (accessed July 2017)
3 Foreword by the Archbishop of Canterbury in G. Tomlin, *Looking Through the Cross: The Archbishop of Canterbury's Lent Book*, London: Bloomsbury, 2013.
4 www.fashion-north.com/index.php/2013/12/05/is-the-cross-becoming-a-fashion-statement/ (accessed July 2017)
5 www.bbc.co.uk/religion/religions/christianity/symbols/cross_1.shtml (accessed July 2017)
6 www.bbc.co.uk/religion/religions/christianity/symbols/cross_1.shtml (accessed July 2017)
7 http://beckhamtattoo.com/david/back/ (accessed July 2017)

CHAPTER 18: THE CROSS IN MODERN ART AND INSTALLATIONS

1 www.glasgowlife.org.uk/museums/kelvingrove/about/collection-highlights/pages/christ-of-st-john-on-the-cross.aspx (accessed June 2017)
2 Quoted in R. Descharnes, *Dalí*, New York: Harry N. Abrams, Inc., 2003.
3 http://uk.complex.com/style/2013/10/chris-burden-art-new-museum/trans-fixed (accessed June 2017)
4 Anderson, C. J., *The Faithful Artist: A Vision for Evangelicalism and the Arts*, Downers Grove, IL: InterVarsity Press, 2016, pp. 67–68.
5 Ibid., p. 68.
6 www.marcusreichert.com/crucifixions.html (accessed June 2017)

CHAPTER 19: THE FUTURE OF THE CROSS

1 For more on the reaction to these controversial murals, see B. Kennedy, et al., *The Hovey Murals at Dartmouth College*, Hanover, NH: Hood Museum of Art & University Press of New England, 2011, p. xiii.
2 Kammen, M., *Visual Shock: A History of Art Controversies in American Culture*, New York: Knopf Doubleday Publishing Group, 2009, p. 135.
3 www.etchings.com/orozco-at-dartmouth.html (accessed May 2017)
4 Rosenthal, P., *The Poets' Jesus: Representations at the End of a Millennium*, Oxford: Oxford University Press, 2000, p. 99.
5 The potential ambivalence regarding the possibility of human progress, as perhaps exemplified in this painting, is stressed in D. M. Coerver, S. B.

Pasztor & R. Buffington, *Mexico: An Encyclopedia of Contemporary Culture and History*, Santa Barbara, CA: ABC-CLIO, 2004, p. 360.
6 President George W. Bush's reference to "this crusade, this war on terrorism", in September 2001, soon set off alarm bells in Europe and was quickly taken up by his opponents in the Middle East. While dropped in favour of the more historically and culturally neutral "war on terrorism", the damage had been done.
7 For this Hadith tradition, see *Mishkat al-Masabih*, J. Robson (trans.), Lahore: Sh. Muhammad Ashraf, 1981, 2:1159.

INDEX

CREDITS

Page 1 Museums of Eastern Funen/Vikingemuseet Ladby; page 11 Collection of Israel Antiquities Authority. Photo © The Israel Museum, Jerusalem by Meidad Suchowolski; page 13 Lebrecht Music & Arts/Alamy Stock Photo; page 16/17 NBC/Getty Images; page 19 Roger Viollet/Getty Images; page 21 Art Collection 3/Alamy Stock Photo; pages 22 and 23 © British Museum; page 24/25 Biblioteca Mediceo Laurenziana, Florence; page 28 Granger Historical Picture Archive/Alamy Stock Photo; page 29 top Copyright © 2000,2001,2002 Free Software Foundation, Inc. 51 Franklin St, Fifth Floor, Boston, MA 02110-1301 USA; page 29 bottom agefotostock/Alamy Stock Photo; page 30 Sputnik/TopFoto; page 32 Print Collector/Hulton Archive/Getty Images; page 33 Copyright © 2000,2001,2002 Free Software Foundation, Inc. 51 Franklin St, Fifth Floor, Boston, MA 02110-1301 USA; page 34 Danita Delimont/Alamy Stock Photo; page 37 Grentidez; page 40 istock/JaimePharr; page 41 British Library, London, UK © British Library Board. All Rights Reserved/ Bridgeman Images; page 42 Reproduced by kind permission of the Chapter of Durham Cathedral; page 44 Bibliothèque municipale de Rouen; page 46 Museums of Eastern Funen/Vikingemuseet Ladby; page 47 Granger Historical Picture Archive/Alamy Stock Photo; page 50 The Picture Art Collection/Alamy Stock Photo; page 54/55 Science History Images/alamy Stock Photo; page 56 The Picture Art Collection/Alamy Stock Photo; page 58/59 Heritage Image Partnership Ltd/Alamy Stock Photo; page 61 DEA PICTURE LIBRARY/Getty Images; page 62 DEA/G. DAGLIORTI/Getty Images; page 63 Print Collector/Hulton Archive/Getty Images; page 64 public domain; page 67 The Walters Art Museum/Creative Commons; page 69 B Christopher/alamy Stock Photo; page 70 Arts of Africa collection/Brooklyn Museum; page 74 Public domain/Museum of Fine Arts Ghent; page 76 The Bodleian Libraries, the University of Oxford, D. 403, fol. 2v; page 77 Museo de Bellas Artes, Valencia/Open Access; page 78 ART Collection/Alamy Stock Photo; page 79 © Victoria and Albert Museum, London; page 81 Oscar Rivera/Quiet Storm Photography; page 83 Yucatan Fine Art Photography/Alamy Stock Photo; page 84 Richard Ellis/Alamy Stock Photo; page 85 National Archives Catalog, USA/Smithsonian Institute; page 86 Private CollectionLook and Learn/Valerie Jackson Harris Collection/Bridgeman Images; page 88 Wigan Arts and Heritage Services; page 89 Gateway Gallery, Hale; page 90 Peter Barrit/Alamy Stock Photo; page 92 Philip Game/alamy Stock Photo; page 95 Library of Congress Prints and Photographs Divison Washington/Wikimedia/public domain; page 96 Sergey Solomko/Wikimedia/public domain; page 97 Walter Kleinfeldt; page 99 Copyright © 2000,2001,2002 Free Software Foundation, Inc. 51 Franklin St, Fifth Floor, Boston, MA 02110-1301 USA; page 100 Popperfoto/ Getty Images; page 101 JERRY/TRIPELON/Getty Images; page 102 ZUMA Press Inc/Alamy Stock Photo; page 103 Fdutil/Wikimedia Commons; page 105 © ADAGP, Paris and DACS, London 2019; page 107 German Federal Archive, Koblenz, Bild 102-15234/cc-BY-SA 3.0; page 108 origo.hu; page 110/111 Uncredited/AP/Shutterstock; page 113 Reproduced by kind permission of the artist, Sushiela Williams; page 115 istock/ Joel Carillet; page 116 © Michael O'Neill McGrath, OSFS/www.bromickeymcgrath.com; page 119 Franck Fotos/Alamy Stock Photo; page 121 Richard Bord/Getty Images Entertainment; page 122 Stephane Cardinale/Corbis Entertainment/Getty Images; page 125 © Julian Simmonds/Telegraph Media Group Limited; page 126 JAVIER SORIANO/AFP/Getty Images; page 129 Brooklyn Museum; page 131 Art Gallery and Museum, Kelvingrove, Glasgow, Scotland © CSG CIC Glasgow Museums Collection/ Bridgeman Images; page 132 Godong/Alamy Stock Photo; page 134 © David Mach; page 135 From the collection of Dr Henry Ralph Carse, Eothen, Huntington, Vermont, USA; page 136/137 Kiev. Victor/ Shutterstock.com; page 139 Baker Library, Dartmouth College, Hanover, NH, USA/Bridgeman Images/ DACS; page 140 Thomas Coex/AFP/Getty Images; page 143 Kumar Sriskandan/Alamy Stock Photo; page 144/145 Tom Pennington/Getty Images News.